Workbook 6

Leading from the Front

Manage Activities
Diploma
S/NVQ Level 5

Institute of Management Open Learning Programme

Series editor: Gareth Lewis
Author: Bob Johnson

the *Institute of Management*
F O U N D A T I O N

**Pergamon
Open
Learning**

Pergamon Open Learning
An imprint of Butterworth-Heinemann
Linacre House, Jordan Hill, Oxford OX2 8DP
225 Wildwood Avenue, Woburn, MA 01801-2041
A division of Reed Educational and Professional Publishing Ltd

ℝ A member of the Reed Elsevier plc group

OXFORD   AUCKLAND   BOSTON
JOHANNESBURG   MELBOURNE   NEW DELHI

First published 1997
Reprinted 1999

British Library Cataloguing in Publication Data
A catalogue record for this book is available from the British Library

ISBN 0 7506 3665 3

Typeset by Avocet Typeset, Brill, Aylesbury, Bucks
Printed and bound in Great Britain

Contents

Series overview

The Institute of Management Open Learning Programme is a series of workbooks prepared by the Institute of Management and Pergamon Open Learning for managers seeking to develop themselves.

Comprising seventeen open learning workbooks, the programme covers the best of modern management theory and practice, and each workbook provides a range of frameworks and techniques to improve your effectiveness as a manager, thus helping you acquire the knowledge and skill to make you fully competent in your role.

Each workbook is written by an experienced management writer and covers an important management topic or theme. The activities both reinforce learning and help to relate the generic ideas to your individual work context. While coverage of each topic is fully comprehensive, additional reading suggestions and reference sources are given for those who wish to study to a greater depth.

Designed to be practical, stimulating and challenging, the aim of the workbooks is to improve performance at work by benefiting you and your organization. This practical focus is at the heart of the competence based approach that has been adopted by the programme.

The structure of the programme

The design and overall structure of the programme has two main organizing principles, both of which are closely linked to the national standards for management developed by the MCI (Management Charter Initiative).

First, the workbooks are grouped according to the key roles of management.

- Underpinning the management standards are a series of **personal competences** which describe the personal skills required by all managers, which are essential to skill in all the main functional or key role areas.
- **Manage Activities** describes the principles of managing processes and activities, with service to the customer as an essential part of this.
- **Manage Resources** describes the acquisition, control and monitoring of financial and other resources.
- **Manage People** looks at the key skills involved in leadership, developing one's staff and managing their performance.

■ **Manage Information** discusses the acquisition, storage and use of information for communication, problem solving and decision making.

In addition, there are three specialized key roles: **Manage Quality, Manage Projects** and **Manage Energy**. The workbooks cover the first two of these. Unlike the four primary key roles above, these are not compulsory for certificate, diploma or S/NVQ requirements, but provide options for the latter.

Together, these key roles provide a comprehensive description of the fundamental principles of management as it applies in any organization – commercial, maintained sector or not-for-profit.

Second, the programme is organized according to **levels of management**, seniority and responsibility.

Level 4 represents first line management. In accredited programmes this is equivalent to S/NVQ Level 4, Certificate in Management or CMS. Level 5 is equivalent to middle/senior management and is accredited at S/NVQ Level 5, Diploma in Management or DMS. There are two S/NVQs at Level 5: Operational Management and Strategic Management. The operations role is focussed internally within an organization on the maintenance of systems and standards of output, whilst the strategic role is focussed on the whole organization, including the external operating environment, and looks at setting directions.

Together, the workbooks cover all the background knowledge you need to have for all units of competence in the MCI standards at Level 4 and Level 5 (apart from the specialized units in the key role Manage Energy). They also provide skills development and opportunities for portfolio building.

For a comprehensive list of workbooks, see page ix. For a comprehensive list of links with the standards, see the *User Guide.*

How to use the programme

The programme is deliberately designed to be flexible and can be used in a variety of ways:

■ to update on important management topics and themes, or develop individual skills: as the workbooks are grouped according to themes, it should be easy for you to pick out one that suits your needs

■ as part of generic management development programmes: you can choose the modules that fit the themes of the programme

■ as part of, and in support of, accredited competence-based programmes.

For N/SVQs at both Levels 4 and 5, there are options in the combinations of units that make up the various awards. By using the map provided in the *User Guide*, individuals will be able to select the workbooks appropriate to their specific needs, and their chosen accreditation options. Some of the activities will help you provide evidence for your portfolio; where we think this is the case, we give the relevant reference to the standards.

For Certificate or CMS, Diploma or DMS, individuals should choose modules that not only meet their individual needs but also satisfy the requirements of the delivering body and the awarding body.

You may need help and guidance in these choices, and the *User Guide* sets out the options and advice in much more detail. A fuller description of the potential uses of this material in evidence gathering and portfolio building can also be found in the *User Guide*, as can a detailed description of the contents of each workbook.

Workbooks in the Institute of Management Open Learning Programme

An asterisk indicates that a particular workbook also contains material suitable for a particular key role or personal competence over and above that where it is principally designated.

Links to qualifications

S/NVQ programmes

This workbook can help candidates to achieve credit and develop skills in the key role of Manage Activities at Level 5, and covers the following units and elements:

A6   Review external and internal operating requirements
A6.1 Analyse your organization's external operating environment
A6.2 Evaluate competitors and collaborators
A6.3 Develop effective relationships with stakeholders
A6.4 Review your organization's structures and systems
A7   Establish strategies to guide the work of the organization
A7.1 Create a shared vision and mission to give purpose to your organization
A7.2 Define values and policies to guide the work of your organization
A7.3 Formulate objectives and strategies to guide your organization
A7.4 Gain support for organizational strategies

Certificate and Diploma programmes

This workbook, together with the other level 5 workbooks on Managing Activities (5 – *Getting TQM to Work* and 7 – *Improving your Organization's Success*), covers all of the knowledge required in the key role managing activities for Diploma and DMS programmes.

Links to other workbooks

Other workbooks in the key role Manage Activities at Level 5 are:

5 *Getting TQM to Work*
7 *Improving your Organization's Success*

and at Level 4:

3 *Understanding Business Process Management*

4 *Customer Focus*

Introduction

The challenge of senior management

Instinctively, few of us are likely to turn down a move into senior management. We may see the offer of such a move as:

- a reward for past success
- recognition of unexploited potential
- resulting from a comparison with other senior managers, which works in our favour
- acknowledgement of our own skills and experience
- the opportunity to prove what we can do

These are likely to be our initial responses. There is nothing wrong with any of them.

Implicit in all of them, though, is the assumption that 'management is management is management'. In other words, that success in a senior management position depends on the effective application of skills and experience gained at the more junior level. The purpose of this workbook is to challenge that assumption.

ACTIVITY I1

How did you feel when you moved into senior management for the first time?

Feeling of achievement & being recognised.

What responsibilities did you expect to face?

*Line management responsibility & for other people's work
Need to make decisions*

How did the reality match up to your expectations?

Line management more frustrating than anticipated.

FEEDBACK

Your first reactions almost certainly included feelings of triumph, elation, of having 'made it'.

You may well have expected that your move into senior management would offer an opportunity to avoid the mistakes you had seen others making at this level – a chance to demonstrate how things should be done.

The reality was probably rather different. Most newly appointed senior managers find themselves facing a new series of challenges for which their past experience has not really equipped them. Suddenly several aspects of the management task look very different:

- decisions need to reflect much longer time-scales
- the impact of actions is much more difficult to predict
- the environment is far less certain
- there is a need to take more account of external factors
- it is still easy to see why past decisions did not work, but not at all easy to find better alternatives for the future
- the workforce expects you to give a clear lead

There are three broad responses to these challenges. The first is for newly appointed senior managers to continue to do the things that have served them well in the past. This is a tempting response, but unlikely to succeed. In the first place, it takes no account of the increased uncertainty and unpredictability involved in the more senior role. In the second place, it leaves a decision-making vacuum at senior level. Many organizations with a traditional hierarchical structure have found that managers who, after promotion, stick with the tried-and-tested approaches they are used to, encroach on the management role of their subordinates. As a result, subordinates find their bosses doing their jobs and more importantly, no one is taking the big decisions. And, finally, the organization lacks the clear direction that will take it successfully into the future.

The second response is precisely the opposite. It assumes that new senior managers are appointed to make a completely fresh start – discarding all ideas and approaches from the past. Of course, for senior managers and their close supporters, this is a stimulating and enjoyable process. But for those on the receiving end, it soon leads to 'change fatigue'. As a Roman centurion wrote home during the first century AD:

No sooner have we become used to the new procedures and learned to apply them effectively than we receive a further set of new instructions which turns everything upside down again.

While there may be sound justifications for revolutionary change, the front-line troops still respond to it with frustration, cynicism and distrust if it happens too often.

The third response effectively involves abdicating responsibility by bringing in outsiders to make the decisions. This may be a matter of bringing in consultants or of recruiting new staff into key positions. Either approach may work. Nevertheless, the result is too often that the organization ends up implementing half-digested textbook solutions, or else importing new approaches that may have been successful elsewhere but which are inconsistent with the needs of the business.

ACTIVITY 12

What experience have you had of:

■ Senior managers doing their subordinates' jobs?

Often – inability to delegate is very common.

What was the result?

Paralysis lower down – inefficient use of human resource

■ A new senior management appointment leading to radical change?

not really leading to radical change.

What was the result?

■ Outsiders being brought in to make the decisions?

None really.

What was the result?

Managing uncertainty

You may have noticed that the senior management standards that this workbook reflects show a marked difference from the junior and middle management standards that precede them. Expressed in slightly simplistic terms, the junior and middle standards are prescriptive – they offer solutions.

By contrast, the senior standards set an agenda – they scope the issues to which solutions need to be found, but without claiming to have all the answers.

That distinction is consistent with several of the themes running through this workbook. The first is that the primary factor that differentiates senior management from management at other levels is the degree of uncertainty which senior managers must handle.

We introduce this theme in Section 1, where we point out in particular that the senior manager's role involves developing internal responses to environmental change. Then, in Section 2, we explore the impact and above all the unpredictability of the external environment. In Sections 3 and 4 we examine changes in the nature of competition and collaboration and draw some tentative conclusions from the current debate about who 'stakeholders' really are.

Our second theme is that of the uniqueness of individual organizations, another factor that makes it unwise to seek universal management panaceas. You will notice that most of the management literature that we quote is tentative in its recommendations. There are frequent references to differences in markets, speed of environmental changes in processes, procedures and the nature of the workforce.

Consequently, when we have quoted examples – from the UK, continental Europe, the USA or Japan – we have tried to make clear the environment in which management decisions were made as well as describing the extent to which they were effective.

Our third theme is the ongoing conflict between the organization's need to adapt and people's need for structure. Thus, while change, responsiveness and flexibility crop up regularly, we have also offered some formal frameworks and procedures – for environmental analysis and internal appraisal in Section 2 and for strategy development in Section 6.

Our final theme is that organizational success depends on commitment and support – but that a high degree of uncertainty stems from the fickleness of that support. The business press is regularly filled with stories of organizations that have come to grief because investors, suppliers or customers have withdrawn their support. And, internally, industrial unrest, strikes and high labour turnover can have a crippling effect on output and efficiency.

In response to this, in Section 4 we examine a range of policies and techniques that can be used to build and maintain shareholder support. Then, in Section 5 we look specifically at the importance of developing a vision for the organization that will not only give it strategic direction, but also fire the imagination and gain the commitment of those on whom the organization depends.

Objectives

By the end of this workbook, you should be able to:

■ define the role of the senior manager

■ explain what differentiates the senior management role from that of other levels

■ analyse the principal external and internal factors which impact on your organization's current and future operating success

■ define the competitive environment in which your organization operates

■ describe current trends in competition and collaboration and their implications for your organization

■ define your organization's stakeholders, their level of commitment and construct an action plan to maintain and increase their support

■ review, develop and gain support for your organization's mission and vision statement

■ construct a strategic plan

■ identify the culture necessary to support that plan

■ recognize the strengths and weaknesses of alternative cultures

Section 1 The role of the manager

The manager as Janus

'You need eyes in the back of your head to be a manager around here.' If you have heard comments such as that in your organization, the implication is probably that the organization itself is an unpredictable and threatening place.

That may be the case. If so, you will find help in several sections of this workbook that focus on ways to develop a strategic direction for the business (and thereby make its activities more predictable) and to gain support from colleagues and staff (and thereby reduce the threat).

In addition, you may want to study *Workbook 8: Project Management* in this series, which concentrates on monitoring and predicting performance in order to take relevant action that will achieve short-term and lont-term improvement. *Workbook 8* will therefore help you to plan more effectively for the future.

However, even if your organization does not seem a particularly unpredictable or threatening place, managers still need eyes in the backs of their heads. In fact, it is part of the manager's role. We can explain this by reference to the god Janus who appears in Roman mythology.

ACTIVITY 1

What do you know about Janus?

Faces both ways - surely important in a senior manager to be able to relate to those above & below in the heirarchy

FEEDBACK

If you have come across Janus, you may know that:

- he was the god after whom the month of January was named
- for the Romans, he was the god of doors and openings
- he is shown as having two faces, pointing in opposite directions

These last two points are the most relevant ones about Janus, both in Roman mythology and for the purposes of this workbook. Having two faces meant that he was able to watch, analyse and respond to two different sets of circumstances, one behind and one in front of him. As the god of openings, he was also associated with new beginnings and opportunities (which is why the first month of the year is named after him) and with exploring unfamiliar territory.

So why is Janus relevant to the role of the manager? See if you can answer that question now in Activity 2.

ACTIVITY 2

Why does a manager need to look in two directions at once? (Think of as many reasons as you can.)

Internal / external audience

~~Strategy~~

Policy / operations

& relations with others as identified previous.

FEEDBACK

There are several reasons you might have come up with. Compare your list with the one below:

- reviewing the past and planning for the future
- fitting the organization to its environment
- representing the organization to its staff and the outside world

REVIEWING THE PAST AND PLANNING FOR THE FUTURE

With the month of January named after him, Janus would have been fully in favour of New Year resolutions! On a personal basis, we review the suitability of past actions and resolve to behave differently in the future. Although we often (always?) break our resolutions, the principle underlying them is that we should learn from what has and has not worked for us in the past and adapt our behaviour so that we respond more effectively to the situations we expect to confront us in the future. In organizational terms, managers are responsible for following the same kind of process by continually applying the control and decision-making cycle shown in Figure 1.

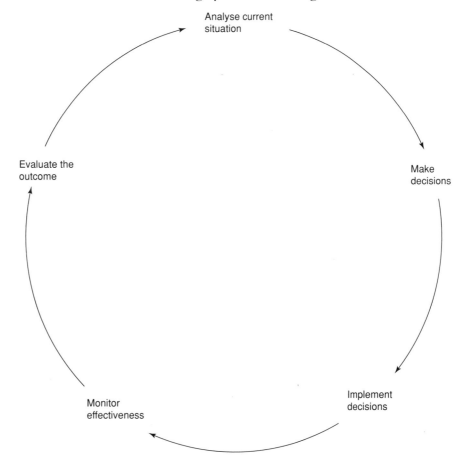

Figure 1   Control and decision-making cycle

Figure 1 shows a circular, iterative process. Effective managers carry out an analysis of the current situation, decide what to do about it, carry out the actions they have decided on, check whether they have worked and then draw general conclusions that they can apply to future situations.

FITTING THE ORGANIZATION TO ITS ENVIRONMENT

In Section 2 of this workbook we shall explore the external environment in which any organization operates. We shall look at, among other things, the political, economic, social, technological, legal and environmental factors which influence or determine the workings of the outside world. However, this environmental analysis is of no value by itself. In order to derive benefit from it, managers need to ask some searching questions about how well the organization fits into both its present and its likely future environment.

We could all enjoy a quieter and less stressful life as managers if all we had to do was focus on the internal efficiency of the organization in which we work. Indeed, for many years, this was seen as the prime objective of civil servants in both local and national government. Of course, this perception was not altogether true even then. It is certainly not true today! Government officials, like all other managers, now have a major responsibility to ensure that the internal workings of the organization – its products, services, financial performance and operating methods – are suited to the needs, wants and expectations of people in the outside world.

As the Figure 2 shows, organizations and the managers working in them must, in order to survive, respond and adapt to a wide variety of influences, opportunities and constraints that all derive from external considerations.

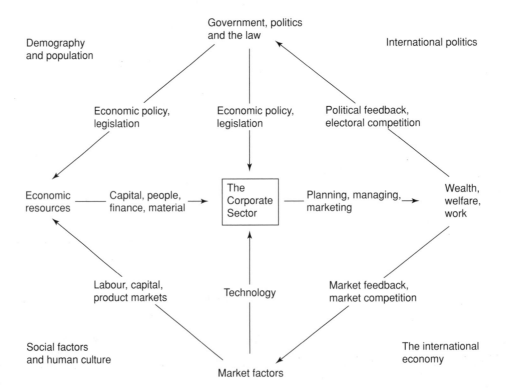

Figure 2   The corporate environment: an analytical framework
(Source: Farnham, 1990)

This is a topic that we shall explore in more detail later.

REPRESENTING THE ORGANIZATION TO ITS STAFF AND THE OUTSIDE WORLD

All staff need confidence in the employer for whom they work. Equally, a wide variety of outside agencies – government, the stock market, consumer bodies, the media and individuals: investors, actual and potential customers, members of the general public – will only invest in, buy from and generally support the organization if they respect and trust it. We shall return to this theme in Section 4 of this workbook.

For the moment, though, we shall consider the contribution of managers to each of these three responsibilities at different levels in an organization.

Looking inside/looking outside

In simple terms, we can summarize these three responsibilities as:

1 internal control and decision making
2 responding to the environment
3 influencing the environment

We have already asserted that all managers have these three responsibilities. However, it is important to recognize that the balance of responsibilities changes as a manager moves upwards through the organization.

Activity 3 asks you to assess the importance of all three at different levels in the organization – and their importance to the job you do currently. For the purposes of the activity, we have split the management function into five levels.

1 **Supervisory** Supervisory managers are typically responsible for a small number of staff (normally operative or clerical) and have limited scope for decision making outside that of day-to-day operations.
2 **Junior** Junior managers have a slightly longer time-span of discretion when it comes to decision making and are likely to be more involved in activities outside their immediate sphere of responsibility.
3 **Middle** Middle managers often have a departmental or functional responsibility and may have other managers reporting to them.
4 **Senior** Senior managers are likely to be involved in both influencing and implementing the strategic direction and objectives of an organization.
5 **Top** Top managers are normally directors. They are responsible for setting the long-term goals and direction of an organization.

Figure 3 which is adapted from Denyer (1972) presents these levels and responsibilities in pictorial form.

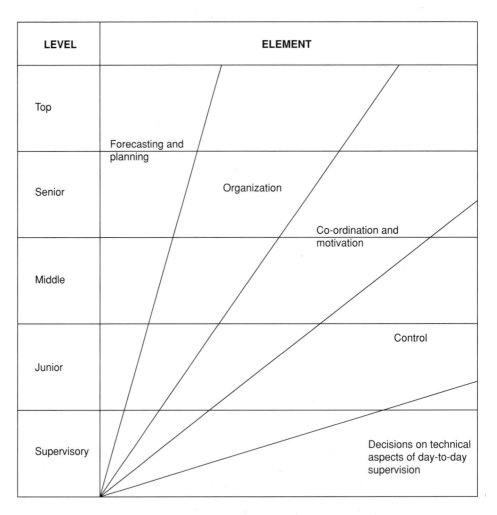

Figure 3 Five levels of management (Source: adapted from Denyer, 1972)

ACTIVITY 3

Think of a specific job at each of the five levels of your organization.

Level	Example job
Top	*Influencing policy makers*
Senior	*Ditto and influencing college principals. Setting direction for directors*
Middle	*Implementing policy*
Junior	*Operational*
Supervisory	*Managing junior staff in routine tasks*

For each of the five levels of management in your organization, give a rating between 0 (no involvement) and 5 (heavy involvement) for the three responsibilities we discussed earlier.

Level	Degree of involvement		
	Internal control and decision making	Responding to the environment	Influencing the environment
Top	4	5	5
Senior	5	5	4
Middle	4	5	4
Junior	3	3	0
Supervisory	3	3	0

FEEDBACK

Of course, we cannot comment specifically on the numbers you have allocated. However, we can offer some comments on the general patterns that we would expect to emerge from an analysis of this kind.

INTERNAL CONTROL AND DECISION MAKING

You probably had some trouble differentiating between types of control and decisions as you moved up the organization. At supervisory and junior levels of management, you probably identified regular and frequent monitoring of work flow, output, levels of attendance and other day-to-day operational issues. At higher levels, the emphasis probably changed to monitoring financial performance on a less frequent basis. And, predictably, control of output would have involved increasingly larger blocks of work as you moved up, still on a regular basis but again less frequently than at a more junior level.

You probably found a similar pattern related to decision making. At lower levels in the organization, decisions were likely to be taken related to ensuring that operations were in line with laid down procedures and a limited amount of day-to-day trouble-shooting, again within fairly tight constraints. As you moved up the organization, you probably found that decisions were increasingly taken with a view to the bigger picture – changing procedures at middle-management level, for example, and longer term, strategic decisions as you moved higher still. Top-level decisions were probably taken less frequently but in a setting of greater uncertainty and with wider implications.

RESPONDING TO THE ENVIRONMENT

You probably found this area of responsibility more straightforward to mark, although even here you may have experienced some difficulties. Typically, managers at lower levels in an organization will have little or no authority to change the way it adapts to its environment. Nevertheless, if your typical supervisory or junior manager carries out a customer-contact role, they may have some responsibility for influencing, if only in a small way, how the organization responds to the outside world, particularly as it relates to individual customers. Equally, the recent adoption by many organizations of the principles of quality management has meant an increasing sensitivity to customer needs, even from non-management grades.

However, the pattern of responsibility you identified in this area almost certainly showed an increasing need to be aware of and respond to environmental demands as you moved up the organization. 'Respond to' are the key words here. Higher level managers are normally better placed in terms of both responsibility and authority to make decisions on how the organization tailors its products and services to the needs of the marketplace, adapts its recruitment practices and reward systems to the expectations of actual and potential employees and adjusts its resourcing requirements to available funding and technological change.

INFLUENCING THE ENVIRONMENT

Earlier, we suggested that the process of influencing the environment involves presenting a positive image of the organization to individuals and bodies both inside and outside. The way you ranked this area of responsibility across the five levels of management almost certainly showed that, at lower levels, managers have significant scope to influence how those *inside* the organization perceive it but far less scope to influence the perception of those outside the organization. Lower levels of management could do little more than influence a few individuals – customers with whom they might have contact, neighbours or people in the pub, for example.

At higher levels, you probably decided that the ability managers had to influence perception was much greater. Since it is principally senior and top managers who determine the culture of an organization, its employment and staff management policies, they are the ones who can have the greatest impact on what staff think about their employer.

CASE STUDY

For many years WH Smith the high street retailer of books and stationery described itself as 'the company where people matter' and 'the caring company'. Consistent with this philosophy most promotion was from within, there was heavy emphasis on the provision of training and development opportunities and it was unheard of for the company to declare redundancies. All the aspects of this philosophy resulted in a general feeling among staff that they enjoyed significant job security and would be generally looked after. Under the pressure of a worsening economic situation, increased competition and a loss of confidence in the investment world, the directors of WH Smith found it necessary to adapt its employment philosophy practices, so that a 'job for life', regular promotion opportunities and an aversion to declaring redundancies all became things of the past. Staff perceptions of the company changed quickly and dramatically.

A similar pattern emerges from a consideration of the scope to influence outside perceptions of the organization.

> ### CASE STUDY
>
> When Gerald Ratner, the boss of Ratner's jewellers in the high street, made an ill-judged comment about the poor quality of the products offered by his company, the results were an almost total loss of confidence among investors, an immediate and catastrophic drop in sales and, ultimately, the take-over of Ratners by H Samuel its principal competitor.

We will summarize the conclusions we can draw from this analysis in the concluding two parts of this section.

Responsible for what?

Colin Coulson-Thomas (1993) identifies a range of attributes and qualities needed by the competent director. His list contains the following:

- personal qualities such as integrity, wisdom, authority, judgement, 'leadership', courage, independence, a positive outlook, tact and diplomacy
- awareness of the business environment and of what constitutes value to customers. (Awareness of developments in the business environment should include ethical and environmental considerations)
- a sense of accountability to stakeholders, and a willingness to put responsibility to the company above self-interest
- vision, and a strategic perspective that should embrace the totality of the company's operations, situation and context
- business acumen and sound commercial judgement
- knowledge of relevant legal and financial issues and requirements. (Particular knowledge is required of the role of the board, and of the legal duties and responsibilities of the directors)
- understanding of the structure and operation of the board, effective boardroom practice, and boardroom matters such as the succession, assessment and remuneration of directors
- skills in such areas as decision making and teamwork in the boardroom context, strategy determination, formulating and achieving objectives, organizing and motivating people, and the monitoring of performance
- experience of relevance to the particular corporate context
- ethical awareness and sensitivity to the attitudes and values of others

The above list is presented in Figure 4.

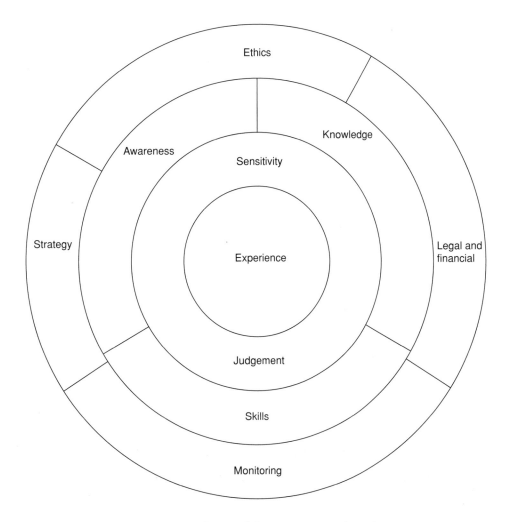

Figure 4 Attributes and qualities of the competent director

Of course, Colin Coulson-Thomas' list of competences is focused on the work of directors. As a result, a number of them, which relate to specific activities in the boardroom, are not relevant to managers working below the top level we have identified.

Nevertheless, we can use his list in two ways. The first is to identify those activities that are the responsibility of senior managers. The second is to analyse the extent to which they are relevant to you and your job. Activity 4 addresses our first question.

ACTIVITY 4

Which of the competences in Colin Coulson-Thomas' list of what he calls 'directorial attributes and qualities' are the responsibility of senior managers? Which are inward-looking and which are outward-looking?

Competence	Senior managers?	Inward-looking?	Outward-looking?
Personal qualities: integrity, wisdom, authority, judgement, leadership, etc	✓	✓	✓
Awareness of the business environment	✓		✓
Sense of accountability to stakeholders	✓		✓
Vision and a strategic perspective	✓		✓
Business acumen	✓		✓
Knowledge of relevant legal and financial issues	✓	✓	
Understanding of the structure and operation of the board			
Skills such as decision making and teamwork, strategy determination, etc.	✓	✓	
Experience relevant to the corporate context	✓		
Ethical awareness	✓	✓	✓

FEEDBACK

Here is our response to Activity 4:

Competence	Senior managers?	Inward-looking?	Outward-looking?
Personal qualities: integrity, wisdom, authority, judgement, leadership, etc	✓	✓	✓
Awareness of the business environment	✓		✓
Sense of accountability to stakeholders	✓	✓	✓
Vision and a strategic perspective	✓	✓	✓
Business acumen	✓	✓	✓
Knowledge of relevant legal and financial issues	✓	✓	✓
Understanding of the structure and operation of the board	✗		
Skills such as decision making and teamwork, strategy determination, etc.	✓	✓	
Experience relevant to the corporate context	✓	✓	✓
Ethical awareness	✓	✓	✓

Your response to the activity may not have been totally consistent with ours. For example, in your organization, strategy determination may be solely the responsibility of the board and you may have interpreted the knowledge of relevant legal and financial issues and requirements as relating purely to the demands of company law.

We believe that Activity 4 highlights two essential points. The first is that, except in the most bureaucratic organizations it is neither possible nor desirable to draw a rigid dividing line between the responsibilities of directors and senior managers for exercising, for example, authority, judgement and leadership and for determining the future direction of the organization.

And, secondly, that at a senior level, managers need to focus, pretty well as much as directors, on the organization's relationship with the external world as much as on the internal workings of the organization.

This point both summarizes and reinforces what we were saying earlier in this section.

Responsible to whom?

The list of directors' responsibilities introduced just now makes a tantalizing reference to 'accountability to stakeholders'. As you completed Activity 4, you will almost certainly have conjured up in your own mind a mental picture of the people who made up this category. Use Activity 5 to formalize that mental picture.

ACTIVITY 5

How would you define the stakeholders in your organization?

Those who have a stake
i.e. college staff, DfEE, ultimately taxpayers

Should have included our staff
How does your organization define them? *& local population*

As above — I think.

FEEDBACK

Your response to that activity will depend on a range of factors:

- how your organization defines its business
- the extent to which your organization is accountable to the general public
- the level of debt which your organization carries and to whom that debt is owed
- your organization's attitude to its staff
- your organization's attitude to its customers or clients
- your organization's dependence on outside agreement to its development plans

Given time, you could probably determine even more factors that would need consideration!

The spectrum of definitions of stakeholders is almost limitless. In a one-man business it could be argued that it is accountable to no one other than its owner-manager. Although, even then it might be advisable to add the owner's immediate family to the group of stakeholders.

In a local authority school, on the other hand, particularly one that has gained financial support from local businesses, it would be sensible to include parents, teachers, students, the community, the Local Education Authority, national government and local businesses among the list of stakeholders.

When you get to Section 4 of this workbook, you will find that we take a broad view of stakeholders, consistent with that presented in the performance standards to which we are working. Our definition will therefore suggest that stakeholders will be made up of any or all of the following:

- shareholders
- customers
- suppliers
- employers
- local and national government
- the general public

There is a significant amount of both academic and practical support for this view. However, it is not the only view. By contrast, some management authors have asserted that the only objective of business is to make profit and that their only stakeholders are therefore the shareholders. Of course, this view is complicated when we consider the people to whom a non profit-making organization is accountable and, in combination with this, what the principal objective of such an organization should be.

For the moment, we will limit ourselves to the observation that, in order to make decisions at a senior level, managers should ensure that those decisions take account of what will be beneficial to their stakeholders in the short term, medium term and long term. And, where there is conflict between these time-frames, the ultimate aim of the organization should be its long-term survival. However, even this assertion is open to debate, as we shall see.

Summary

In this first section we have examined the role of the senior manager. Just as management is different from other professional disciplines, so the role of senior manager is different from that of junior and middle management, and much of that difference centres on the contribution to strategy and business planning.

In this section we have covered:

- the differences between senior management and other levels of management
- the three key responsibilities of internal control and decision making; responding to the environment; influencing the environment
- the attributes, qualities and competences of senior managers

Section 2   Looking outside – the external environment

'Baby, it's cold outside'

In Section 1, we encouraged you to recognize a progression in management levels by which, as they move up the organization, managers become less involved in managing day-to-day internal or operational issues and increasingly involved in considering both the impact of internal decisions on the outside world and that of the external environment on internal actions.

In philosophical terms, you may have had little difficulty in accepting the consequences of this progression. In practical and emotional terms, however, most managers find this change in thinking very problematic.

ACTIVITY 6

In your view, and based on your experience why would managers have difficulty in changing their thinking in this way? (There may be several reasons.)

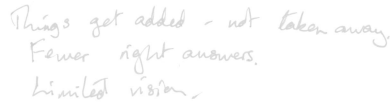

Things get added - not taken away.
Fewer right answers.
Limited vision.

FEEDBACK

We identified the following reasons:

- the pressure of conditioning
- fear of the unknown
- the wish to conform

THE PRESSURE OF CONDITIONING

By 'conditioning', we mean the way our past experience influences the way we think today. Think, for example, about the first management job you ever did. You were probably concerned about – even terrified by – the technical content of the job. For the first time, you were being expected, not just to solve your own problems, but to give expert advice to help your team solve their problems as well. Almost certainly, that expertise related to internal factors – the products, the systems, the services, the other people in the organization. You may have been on the odd management course, where you were trained to plan, organize, direct and control (if the course was based on classical management theory) or else to communicate, motivate and delegate (if the course had 'the manager as leader' as its main emphasis).

We are not suggesting that there is anything wrong with any of these early management experiences. On the contrary, we have already seen that relevant technical expertise, the ability to lead, motivate and build teams are as necessary to senior managers as to those in more junior management positions. Unfortunately, for junior managers, the focus in most cases is exclusively internal. Their teams' expectations of them emphasize the manager's responsibility to lead and provide technical expertise and guidance. The organization's expectations are that managers will ensure conformity to the standards, systems and procedures of the organization. As a result, many managers spend their formative years learning the internal workings of the organization, with little or no recognition of the world outside its walls.

FEAR OF THE UNKNOWN

At a simplistic level, 'fear of the unknown' merely means that if junior managers have not been conditioned to respond to the outside world, then such a process will seem impossibly daunting when they move to a more senior position.

However, this is less than half the story. In a research study published in 1956, Norman Martin reported on the types of decisions taken by four different levels of management in a US manufacturing company.

Dr Martin identified among other things, the fact that decisions taken at a junior level were:

... much more clear cut. What had to be done was more easily seen, it usually had to be done quickly and there was less uncertainty about the result than at higher levels. At the higher levels the decision situation was much more indefinite; the time within which action should be taken was often indeterminate as it could depend upon the judgement of the total situation; what should be done was often difficult to decide because there were so many elements of uncertainty in the decision.

Faced, then, with the challenge of responding to the outside world, where the situation is complex, confusing, uncertain and unpredictable, it is not surprising that even senior, experienced managers prefer the comfort of the known.

THE WISH TO CONFORM

The American occupational psychologist, Irving L. Janis, coined the term 'groupthink' to describe the process by which members of an organization come to believe that the organization is always right and totally invulnerable. Under the influence of groupthink, all decisions taken by the organization are seen as the right decisions, simply because the organization has taken them.

Groupthink provides a further incentive to disregard the complexities of the external world, because it brings with it the implication that the wider environment is largely irrelevant to the organization. After all, if the organization is invulnerable and decisions are always right by definition, there is little point in thinking too much about their impact on the external world.

If managers are conditioned to focus internally and decisions related to the environment are fraught with uncertainty, the temptation to rely on the organization as all-wise and all-powerful becomes very strong.

Nevertheless, as we shall see, the speed and unpredictability of change threaten the survival of all organizations. Managers at all levels, but particularly in senior positions, have a duty to monitor and respond appropriately to environmental change. There is nothing new in this. All that has changed is the speed with which the unexpected arrives and the consequent need to be perpetually vigilant.

Monitoring change

The management literature of the 1970s, 1980s and 1990s has been full of titles by authors highlighting the impact and speed of changes in the environment and the need for organizations to respond appropriately to them.

The American author John Naisbitt, in his books, *Megatrends* (1984) and *Re-inventing the Corporation*, stressed the changes from an industrial to an information society, from a national to a world economy, from centralized to decentralized structures, from hierarchies to networks. He advocated responses involving longer term planning, a need for individuals to take greater responsibility for their own futures and a move from either/or to more complex decision making.

Charles Handy, writing in the UK in his books such as *The Future of Work*, *The Age of Unreason* and *The Empty Raincoat* has emphasized the need for society to redefine its view of work and has promoted a vision of organizations far removed from traditional hierarchical structures.

Tom Peters, in, among other titles *Thriving on Chaos* (1988) and *Liberation Management* has stressed the speed of change and the need for organizational responses that are speedy, creative, often revolutionary and above all not bounded by tradition.

However, the principal task of the literature to which we have referred is that environmental change is obvious, if only we are open to it. This may be true on a large scale, but the process of identifying the nature of the environment in which organizations operate also requires a structured, disciplined approach. We shall consider that now.

Traditionally, the environmental factors to which organizations are subject have been summarized under the acronym PEST, standing for:

Political
Economic
Social
Technological

More recently, the recognition of the growing impact of the Law and Environmental (or 'green') issues have led to an alternative and rather clumsier acronym PESTLE.

The political environment

ACTIVITY 7   A6.1

What political pressure is your organization subject to?

Government.   A B C

How exposed are you to political decisions at an international level?

International Limited

How exposed are you to political decisions at a national level?

Very

How exposed are you to political decisions at a local level?

Limited but will increase with LSC

What changes do you expect in international politics that may affect you?

What changes do you expect in national politics that may affect you?

Establishment LSC

What changes do you expect in local politics that may affect you?

How do you access information about the political environment in which your organization operates?

Press discussion with colleagues

What does your organization do to monitor the political environment?

Press, briefings etc.

How is the resulting information disseminated?

FEEDBACK

Of course, since these questions all relate directly either to you or to your organization, we cannot comment specifically on your answers. However, the following points may help you to develop and clarify your thinking.

In 1997 some of the key developments in the political environment are:

■ Bill Clinton has just been sworn in as the new President of the United States

His new administration faces significant questions related to international trade, taxation, levels of employment and healthcare. All of these have commercial implications.

■ Great Britain returns Hong Kong to Chinese control

Many countries which currently trade with, or have branches in, Hong Kong are waiting to see whether the Chinese government will continue to promote the island as a major international trading centre. It could become the gateway to trade with China, or alternatively be required to adopt a more isolationist stance.

- **The government of Slobodan Milosevic in Serbia has overturned the results of some local elections, leading to popular protests and significant international disapproval**

National Westminster, the UK bank, has withdrawn from a consultancy project to advise on restructuring Serbia's national debt and is under pressure to cease involvement with the privatization of the country's postal and telecommunications system.

- **New Government in the UK**

The main political parties all have different views on the UK's entry into the European Monetary Union. As a result, companies trading with Europe have to address the uncertainty and the opportunities. In addition, the new government will face major questions about healthcare, pensions, adoption of the Social Chapter, taxation and education. All of these have political implications.

- **Local government in the UK is predominantly Labour and Liberal Democrat**

However, their budgets are under tight control from Westminster. Harmony between local and national government – and, almost certainly, the level of funding available for local initiatives – is dependent on the party in power at Westminster.

This brief summary has done no more than emphasize the extent to which decisions about investment, marketing, trading and personnel practices are strongly under the influence of political decisions at international, national and local levels.

It is therefore true to say that managers need to monitor political trends – through the media, business associations, local chambers of commerce and networking outside the organization. The culture of the organization should encourage this access to political intelligence by supporting memberships of relevant associations, promoting links with individuals and bodies outside the organization, subscribing to relevant journals and even actively extracting and circulating articles on a regular basis.

The economic environment

How subject is your organization to the international economy?

Only in the sense that UK plc is

How is the economy performing in the individual countries where you trade?

N/A OK in UK

What are the implications of that performance for you?

N/A more money to colleges

What are the differences in economic performance between the different local regions where you trade?

What are the implications of that performance for you?

What action do you take to monitor economic performance at these three levels?

FEEDBACK

As before, we cannot comment specifically on your answers. However, you may find these general points useful.

THE INTERNATIONAL ECONOMY

Your organization may not trade internationally. But your customers or clients may do. Consequently, if you operate in a business-to-business environment, you will almost certainly be subject to the impact of the international economy on those customers.

That impact may be less marked in retail or consumer markets. Nevertheless, even here, your customers may work for organizations that are themselves involved in international trade. A buoyant international economy will increase their confidence and buying power, while a depressed international economy will have the opposite effect. Equally, the international economy may affect the products and marketing effort of overseas competition.

THE NATIONAL ECONOMY

If you trade in different countries overseas, it will be important to track the relative strength or weakness of the different economies. You may decide to divert your marketing effort from a weak to a strong economy, where confidence and buying power are greater. Or you may choose to divert your effort in the opposite direction.

CASE STUDY

Coutts Career Consultants, the UK-based outplacement business, recognized that the upturn in the UK economy in the mid-1990s meant that client organizations would have less need to make staff redundant, particularly as many clients had already completed major down-sizing initiatives. As a response, Coutts acquired an outplacement business in France, where the economic downturn had started later and was predicted to continue.

Even if you trade exclusively in your home economy, the strength or weakness of that economy will have significant implications for the cost of labour, the cost of raw materials, customer confidence and willingness to buy or invest, as well as for pricing policy and the attractiveness of basic or more sophisticated goods and services.

THE LOCAL OR REGIONAL ECONOMY

Retailers provide the classic example of the importance of responding to local economic conditions. At a primary level, the decision whether to open a new store will be influenced by, among other factors, the current and predicted future state of customer confidence and buying power.

At a more sophisticated level, decisions on product ranges will be taken to reflect what customers in a particular locality are likely to want and be able to afford. For example, Marks and Spencer, the UK clothing retailer, limits its high-priced fashion items to a selected range of stores, one of which predictably, is in London's Oxford Street.

MONITORING ECONOMIC INDICATORS

The first question we should ask is:

■ What economics indicator might you need to monitor?

See if you can answer that question now in Activity 9.

ACTIVITY 9   A6.1

What economic indicators might you monitor:

Internationally?

Nationally?

Locally?

FEEDBACK

In order to monitor the **international** economy, you might have mentioned any or all of the following indicators:

■ comparative rates of inflation
■ comparative movements in stock prices across the major stock markets
■ price movements for raw materials, precious metals or commodities
■ movements in retail prices
■ wage rates
■ Gross Domestic Product
■ per capita consumption

You may have identified other indicators more relevant to your own line of business. The important point to recognize is that data of this kind provide a valuable picture of the international economy because they enable a comparison between countries.

At a **national** level, similar indicators apply, but this time their value derives from comparisons over time, which allow you to identify trends in economic performance and make predictions about where these trends are likely to lead.

Locally, comparisons are still important. This time, though, as we have suggested, it may be helpful to compare economic performance across different regions, in order to highlight the relative attractiveness of local markets.

The sources of such data are many and varied. They range from government publications such as the UK's *Employment Gazette* or the Central Stationery Office's *Monthly Digest of Statistics* to international publications such as the IMF's *International Financial Statistics*, to local government data, information from local Chambers of Commerce or national trade associations.

ACTIVITY 10   A6.1

What sources of economic data are relevant to the business of your organization?

Who could you ask to help you extend your list?

The social environment

The study of the social environment is often known as demographics. It deals with such aspects as (to quote the old joke) people broken down by age and sex, numbers of people in a family, lifestyle, buying preferences and behaviour, the age and sex of breadwinners, educational qualifications and the age at which people left full-time education. Such information is available for countries, regions and, increasingly, for more restricted populations at a local neighbourhood level. For example, the ACORN classification (standing for A Classification of Residential Neighbourhoods) is extensively used by retailers to identify the different housing types in a local area, from which can be derived their buying power, level of sophistication, attitudes to different products and services (from brown sauce to package holidays).

ACTIVITY 11

How important are demographic trends to your organization?

Important to colleges e trainers

How do you use demographic information?

Demographic trends and data are used for such diverse purposes as:

- establishing whether a specific location would support a particular retail outlet
- predicting the future need for a school
- analysing the type and volume of healthcare needed in a local community
- assessing whether a town needs more car parks or more public transport

The technological environment

You will already have noticed that, while we have attempted to treat environmental factors separately, they are in fact more like interlocking rings, each having an impact on others.

Nowhere is this more true than in the impact of technological change. For example, it has been argued that the greatest factor contributing to the breakdown of family life was the advent of central heating systems that allowed different members of the family to do their own thing comfortably in the isolation of separate rooms.

Arguably, technological change has had a greater impact on organizational life than that of any other environmental factor.

ACTIVITY 12   A6.1

What impact has technological change had in your organization:

On products and services?

On systems?

On operating methods?

On working patterns?

We will highlight just a few examples of the impact of technological change on organizational life.

PRODUCTS AND SERVICES

The invention of the internal combustion engine, to quote Theodore Levitt's (1975) famous example from his article 'Marketing Myopia' in the *Harvard Business Review*, led ultimately to the demise of the buggy whip industry.

The increasing use of microchips in a wide range of consumer durable products has made them more versatile. But it has also led to a revolution in maintenance and servicing. Where once service engineers prodded, poked, listened and adjusted, they will now plug-in a diagnostic tool, read off details of the malfunctioning part, remove it and fit a new one.

SYSTEMS

The obvious examples under this heading result from the increasing use of computers. Data storage, analysis, manipulation and transfer are all both easier and faster. However, as this technology has become more sophisticated, and its use more essential to communication so it has become necessary to introduce back-up systems and to cope with the sheer volume of paper which computers generate. As a result, new industries have grown up which provide microfiche storage, off-site warehousing and bomb-proof vaults.

OPERATING METHODS

We have already mentioned the change to servicing procedures resulting from the introduction of the microchip. Some other technological innovations which we take for granted – such as the photocopier, the fax and the mobile phone – have not only revolutionized communication and paperwork but also had a major and negative impact on suppliers of traditional products and services such as carbon paper and the postal system.

WORKING PATTERNS

Improvements in communication technology have also contributed to the phenomenon commonly known as teleworking. As organizations in the post-industrial society rely less on operatives and more on knowledge workers, so it has become increasingly popular for people to work from home, either permanently or with occasional visits to a central location for essential meetings.

This social change, which is significant in itself, has also:

- reduced commuting
- led to a decline in the need for city-centre office accommodation
- encouraged more women back to work
- raised important questions about the workplace as a social forum

The legal environment

The philosophy of the former Conservative government during its three terms of office in the UK has been to encourage freedom and competitiveness by reducing the constraints under which organizations operate. The practice, however, has been rather different. Consumer groups have sought greater protection for customers; membership of the EC has made organizations liable to greater controls over product safety and employment practices. The recent tragedy of the Dunblane massacre, meanwhile, has led to new legislation related to the use, ownership and safe storage of firearms.

The extent to which the state should control individuals and organizations in society is a contentious and largely political issue. However, the two implications contained in that statement – that there is some need for control in society and that the state has some part to play in exercising it – are fundamental to any definition of law.

Bardshaw and Palfreman (1986) quote these definitions of law by well-known jurists:

The body of principles recognised and applied by the State in the administration of justice. ... In other words the law consists of rules recognised and acted upon by courts of justice (Salmond)

A law is a general rule of external human action enforced by a sovereign political authority (Holland)

A social process for settling disputes and securing an ordered existence in the community (Paton)

We do not have the space here to examine in detail the full scope of the laws to which your organization may need to conform. Legal textbooks normally run to several hundreds of pages and usually stress that, since English law is derived, not only from statute but also from precedents set by individual cases, all interpretations must be provisional. As a result, we have not attempted to describe in full the obligations which the law places on organizations.

However, the next activity lists just some of the laws that may affect you and your organization. Activity 13 involves consideration of two questions:

1 Which of these laws are significant for your organization?
2 Would it be helpful for you to know more about the content of any of them?

ACTIVITY 13   A6.1

Complete this activity by ticking the appropriate columns.

Statute	Relevant	Need to know more
Betting, Gaming and Lotteries Act 1963		
Bills of Exchange Act 1982		
Building Act 1984	✓	
Business Names Act 1985		
Cheques Act 1957		
Civil Liability (Contribution) Act 1978		
Companies Acts 1985 and 1989		
Company Directors (Disqualification) Act 1986		

Statute	Relevant	Need to know more
Company Securities (Insider Dealing) Act 1985		
Consumer Credit Act 1974		
Consumer Protection Act 1987		
Consumer Safety Act 1978		
Copyright Act 1956		
Data Protection Act 1984	✓	
Defective Premises Act 1972	✓	
Employers Liability Act 1969	✓	
Employment Acts 1980, 1988, 1989	✓	
Employment Protection (Consolidation) Act 1978	✓	
Equal Pay Act 1970	✓	
Factories Act 1937 and 1961	✓	
Fair Trading Act 1973		
Finance Act 1929		
Financial Services Act 1936		
Food Act 1984		
Gaming Act 1845		
Health and Safety at Work Act 1974	✓	
Hire Purchase Act 1964		
Insolvency Act 1986		
Law Reform Acts 1934, 1943, 1945		
Misrepresentation Act 1967		
Office, Shops and Railways Premises Act 1964	✓	
Pharmacy and Poisons Act 1933		
Prevention of Fraud Acts 1939, 1956		
Race Relations Act 1976	✓	
Rehabilitation of Offenders Act 1974	✓	
Resale Prices Act 1976		
Restriction of Offensive Weapons Acts 1959,1961		
Restrictive Trade Practices Acts 1976 and 1977		
Sales of Goods Acts 1893 and 1979		
Sex Discrimination Acts 1975 and 1986		
Social Security Acts 1985, 1986		
Social Security Pensions Act 1975		
Supply of Goods and Services Act 1982		
Supply of Goods (Implied Taxes) Act 1973		
Tools (Interface with Goods) Act 1977		
Trade Descriptions Act 1968		
Trade Union and Labour Relations Act 1974		
Unfair Contract Terms Act 1977		
Unsolicited Goods and Services Act 1976		
Wages Act 1986		
Weights and Measures Act 1985		

FEEDBACK

This list of Acts, extensive though it is, does not exhaust the full range of statutes to which organizations are subject.

If you would like to know more about any of them, or about those which we have excluded for reasons of their obscurity, we suggest you refer to *Business Law* by Denis Keenan and Sarah Riches.

The 'green' environment

If we go right back to the period of the enlightenment in the eighteenth century, we find a philosophy based on the idea that, with proper care and effort, humankind is capable of not only understanding the material world, but adapting and improving it, to the benefit of the human population.

This principle of the material world given to us as raw material to be fashioned to our needs underpins much business activity in the nineteenth and early twentieth century. Progress and improvements were the two watchwords.

Only in the latter half of this century have people come to recognize the destructive effects they were having on the environment. And so, along with the recognition that humankind maybe did not have all the answers, came the 'green' movement with its emphasis on avoiding damage to the natural world and repairing it wherever possible.

ACTIVITY 14   A6.1

What consequences of the 'green' movement can you think of?

FEEDBACK

You may have mentioned:

- the introduction of unleaded petrol
- the search for alternatives to CFCs in refrigerators
- protests against road-building schemes
- the drive for improved and subsidized public transport
- protests against the fur and ivory trades
- decline in support for nuclear energy
- the search for renewable energy sources
- recycled paper and packaging
- growth in cycle tracks
- increased emphasis on home insulation

ACTIVITY 15   A6.1

What impact has the 'green' movement had on your organization?

Recycling!

What future effects do you expect it to have?

Reduced use of paper
Flexible working

FEEDBACK

We cannot comment directly on your answer. However, we would expect you to have made some reference depending on your business to:

- raw materials used in your products
- manufacturing processes
- greater attention to reducing waste
- increased concern about office and factory design
- a re-evaluation of transport policy
- rethinking of office and factory locations
- recycling land and materials rather than using new

As we shall see in Section 4 of this workbook, the purpose of this greater concern for the environment is not limited to the fulfilment of organizational ethics. Rather, it is an important consideration in attracting staff (tobacco and oil exploration companies find it difficult to do so without offering a significant premium) and in maintaining and building customer loyalty (coffee companies who are seen to exploit native workers and abuse the environment find that customers vote with their purses).

Summary

In this section we have looked at the external environment of the organization, and why it is important to analyse its components.

Specifically, we have covered:

- the rationale for external environmental analysis
- attitudes and approaches to change
- analysis of external environment through political, economic, social, technological, legal and environmental factors

Section 3   With us or against us

The nature of competition

We need to distinguish between an economist's definition of competition and the one we use more commonly in organizations.

For the economist:

A perfectly competitive market is one in which both buyers and sellers believe that their own buying or selling divisions have no effect on the market price (Begg, Fischer and Dornbush, 1984)

J.K. Galbraith (1988) spells out the practical implications of this:

If any seller asks more than the market price, then all customers can go to those who sell at the market price. They are a readily available alternative. The presence or total withdrawal of any one seller or any one buyer doesn't appreciably alter the price in the market. So there is nothing any one buyer or seller can do to influence the market.

ACTIVITY 16

How do these economic definitions of competition square with the industry in which your organization operates?

FEEDBACK

You probably identified some marked differences! You may have decided, for example, that:

- the product or service you offer is significantly, or at least, slightly, different from those offered by your competitors
- you, or a competitor, are big enough for your presence in, or absence from, the market to make a difference to the overall level of prices
- your customers' choice in the marketplace is limited, possibly by geographical location or by other factors affecting the convenience of access

For the economist, perfect competition depends on:

- all firms making essentially the same product, for which they must all charge the same price
- the buyers having almost perfect information about the characteristics of the products being sold so that they know the products of different firms in a competitive industry really are identical
- the presence of a large number of firms in the industry, so that each is trivial relative to the industry as a whole
- free entry to and exit from the market, so that, even if existing firms could organize themselves to restrict total supply and drive up the market price, the consequent increase on revenues and profits would simply attract new firms into the industry, thereby increasing total supply again and driving the price back down. Conversely, when firms in a competitive industry are losing money, some firms will close down and, by reducing the number of firms remaining in the industry, reduce the total supply and drive the price up.

Clearly, there are few, if any, industries to which all these factors apply. As we shall see later in this section, there is a major trend in the direction of a few very big firms in the marketplace, producers compete by differentiating their products or services from those of their competitors, the complexity of differentiated products and services makes it difficult for buyers to obtain perfect information about them and the process of entry to and exit from the market is complicated by the time, resources and expense involved in making such a move.

The conclusion we can draw from all this is that, although western democracies pride themselves on being free market economies, with a high level of competition, the real situation is distinctly different from what the economists mean when they use these terms.

So let us turn to a marketing definition of competition. Marshall C. Howard (1964) explains the marketing viewpoint as follows:

The producer–seller must satisfy the customers' wants. To do this he must know the customers' wants and be able to satisfy them as well as or better than business rivals can. Competition can be in terms of price, quality, nature of the product or service, or conditions of sale. The successful producer–seller is the one who has been most skilful in researching the buyers' wants, in procuring the resources to satisfy those wants, and in promoting sales. Other things being equal, this is accomplished by offering the best-quality goods at the lowest prices and on the most convenient terms of sale and delivery. Competition forces the business rivals to provide the best for the least. The efficient firms will be profitable and survive; the inefficient will not.

So far, so simple. Just about all definitions of marketing stress that it is a process whereby suppliers identify and satisfy customer needs and wants. However, the reality is much more complicated. In the saturated markets of today, as we shall explore in more detail later, it is rare to be able to identify a major customer need that is genuinely unsatisfied. The history of product and service innovation is strewn with examples of revolutionary inventions that never made it – the Sinclair C7 three-wheeler, for example, and nicotine-free cigarettes.

Consequently, the most that suppliers can do generally is to introduce minor improvements into the marketplace in the hope that these will be sufficient to make the product or service more attractive than those of the competition. And, in most cases, this minor advantage will be short-lived. If it succeeds, competitors will copy or refine it. Ironically, it is this process that brings the real marketplace closest to the economists' definition of an undifferentiated product as one of the four factors constituting perfect competition.

It should also be recognized that the identification of an unsatisfied need, even if that were possible, does not automatically result in a successful product or service. Firms in the marketplace are competing for a finite amount of consumer spending power. Consequently, the purchase of a new product or service usually depends on a decision to go without something that is currently bought. This means that the new product is a displacement purchase and needs to offer advantages that outweigh the loss of those offered by the displaced product.

This brings us onto the subject of product substitution. A Parker pen, for example, might be seen to be in competition with other pens from Cross or Waterman. However, a Parker pen is often bought as a present. Consequently, it is actually competing with any other product that might be seen as attractive to the intended recipient – a lighter, a CD, or even a theatre ticket.

ACTIVITY 17

Who would you define as your competitors?

Eg TSC / FEDA / TECs / LEAs depending on what function.

How clearly are your products and services differentiated from those of your competitors?

Determined by govt in general.

What product displacement, if any, would be necessary to allow increased sales of your products or services?

N/A

What are the substitutes for your products and services?

Full cost programmes.

So far, we have asked you to carry out a very broadbrush evaluation of your competitors. Of course, in practical terms you need to go much further than this. Hugh Davidson (1987) offers the following checklist of competitive advantage:

How does your organization compare with its competitors from the viewpoint of:

Superior product benefit

■ better end result
greater convenience
superior service
longer lasting
more features
superior product design
better in-use characteristics

Focus on niche positioning

- strong appeal to minority segment

Perceived customer advantage

- built on imagery rather than function

Lower cost operator

- low-cost operations
- low-cost distribution
- low-cost overheads

Superior knowledge

- segmentation, processes, systems, R&D
- superior allocation of resources

Stronger contacts

- key customers
- innovative licensers or licences
- joint venture partners

Scale advantages

- market position
- branding strength
- product range
- advertising spend
- sales force/distribution muscle
- raw material sourcing/control
- financial muscle
- operations/processing

Legal advantages

- patent protection
- exclusive/protected rights
- protective legislation/practices
- copyright

Company attitudes

- e.g. long-term orientation

International trends in competition and collaboration

There are two truisms in international marketing:

1 the obvious growth in importance of international and multinational organizations
2 the increasing globalization of markets

However, the overall international picture is less straightforward than these two, apparently simple, trends may suggest.

DOES THE GLOBAL MARKET REALLY EXIST?

For almost twenty years, a debate has raged over whether it is possible to treat the world as a single market. In an article in 1983, Theodore Levitt argued that:

The globalization of markets is at hand. With that, the multinational commercial world nears its end, and so does the multinational corporation. The multinational and the global corporation are not the same. The multinational corporation operates in a number of countries, and adjusts to its products and practices in each – at high relative costs. The global corporation operates with resolute constancy – at low relative cost – as if the entire world (or major regions of it) were a single entity; it sells the same things in the same way everywhere. Which strategy is better is not a matter of opinion but of necessity.

This is not the only view, however, P. M. Chismall (1977) points out that:

Superficially, modern cities over the world tend to look alike: the modern 'super culture' .... built upon the culture of airports, throughways, skyscrapers and artificial fertilisers, birth control and universities (may look the same the world over), but beneath the surface, cultural shackles may not be loosened as easily as old buildings are demolished.

The implication of this view is that linguistic, religious, cultural, technological and legal differences between countries effectively preclude standardization, except in rare cases in which a high degree of similarity in market conditions, consumer attitudes and product benefits exists.

Different organizations have espoused these two opposing views, with varying degrees of success. Both Schweppes International and Coca-Cola have achieved success with consistent, international brands. Fiat, on the other hand, found that cars with basic equipment levels, with which they successfully dominated the Italian market, did not compete effectively in the UK with much more highly equipped Japanese models – and were forced to update the specification.

The conclusion to be drawn from this debate is that, while it is important for organizations to take advantage, where possible, of the economies of scale available from global operations, it remains essential to recognize the difference in culture, environment and customer needs of different countries – and to adapt accordingly. In terms of competition, this means avoiding the mistaken belief that customers and competitors will respond in the same way as in the home country and ensure that global decisions are based on accurate local information. From the point of view of collaboration, it may be necessary to establish close working relationships with overseas partners, in order to benefit from their local knowledge and expertise.

Localization of production

While markets are becoming increasingly global, the opposite trend is influencing production. Kurtz and Boone (1981) explain the phenomenon:

An understanding of the concepts of absolute and comparative advantage is vital to the study of world marketing. These concepts explain why countries specialise in the marketing of certain products. A nation has an absolute advantage in marketing of a product if it is the sole producer or can produce the product for less than anyone else. Since few nations are sole producers, and since economic conditions rapidly alter production costs, examples of absolute advantage are rare. The concept of comparative advantage is a more practical approach to international trade specialisation. Under this concept, a nation has a comparative advantage in an item if it can produce it more efficiently than it can produce alternative products. Nations usually produce and export those goods in which they have the greatest comparative advantage (or the least comparative disadvantage) and import those items in which they have the least comparative advantage (or the greatest comparative disadvantage).

It is this phenomenon, specifically related to technological innovation, wage costs and productivity, which explains the Japanese domination of the electronic goods market. By the same token, though, it also explains the transfer of manufacturing by Japanese firms to the Pacific Rim countries, as their own wage costs have risen. The less successful example of this process is the emphasis, under the Thatcher government in the UK, on a move from manufacturing to service industries.

The lesson for competition here is the need to identify the competitive advantages available from a careful exploitation of national strengths and differences. As far as collaboration is concerned, it means finding partners in other countries who can complement your own home strengths.

Trends in collaboration

Rosabeth Moss Kanter (1989) sets the scene for this topic:

In the face of heightened competitive pressures and the world-wide scope of both technology and markets, many US firms have established new co-operative agreements with other organizations at home and abroad that involve unprecedented (for them) levels of sharing and commitment. While American firms, particularly small ones, have always allied with other firms for specific purposes, the extent as well as the diversity of such activity has grown in recent years, moving from the periphery to take a central place in some companies' strategies. Indeed, international alliances and partnerships are associated with competitive strength: entered into by larger firms, by those more experienced internationally, and in strategically important industries by those with strong domestic positions.

The arguments in favour of increased and closer collaboration are:

- faster access to resources and expertise
- greater incentive to innovate
- more effective response to technological change
- greater flexibility
- improved security for the small partner

Collaborative alliances can take one of three forms:

- **Service alliances**   Where a group, or consortium, of organizations with a similar need, often in the same industry, band together to fill that need for all of them. It may be for the purpose of research and development, to provide a service such as distribution or insurance needed by all, or to generate greater marketing or purchasing power.
- **Opportunistic alliances**   This is where organizations see an opportunity to gain an immediate though perhaps temporary, competitive advantage through an alliance that gives them access to a new business, or extends an old business. The two principal driving forces behind this kind of alliance are competence-enhancing ones: technology transfer or market access or both. Rover's alliance with Honda to provide new models and engines is an example of an opportunistic alliance, providing Rover with access to the design and Honda with improved access to the market.
- **Stakeholder alliances**   As we shall explain in more detail in Section 4 of this workbook, stakeholder alliances involve redefining supplier relationships. Instead of maintaining an 'arm's length' relationship with a variety of suppliers, based primarily on price, stakeholder alliances recognize the mutual dependence of customer and supplier. They result in a smaller number of suppliers, with greater emphasis on quality, joint problem solving and innovation.

ACTIVITY 18

Does your organization operate internationally?

If so, does it take a global or a multinational approach?

Is this approach consistent with the extent of differences between individual markets?

Does your organization take advantage of the comparative advantages of various supplier nations?

If not, how could this be improved?

What kinds of alliances is your organization involved in?

Are you satisfied with the results of those alliances?

If not, how could they be improved?

Free markets, monopolies and oligopolies

Let us start with some definitions:

Free markets are markets in which governments do not intervene. Individuals in free markets pursue their own interests, trying to do as well for themselves as they can without any government assistance or interference. Free markets are as close as we get to perfect competition although, as we have seen, this situation is rarely achieved.

In a **monopoly**, there is a sole supplier and potential supplier of the industry's product. The form and the industry coincide. There is no competition.

Typically, monopolies are either state-run or government-regulated in an attempt to ensure availability of the product or service and to control prices.

An **oligopoly** is an industry with only a few producers, each recognizing that its own price depends not merely on its own output but also on the actions of its important competitors in the industry.

ACTIVITY 19   A6.2

How would you define the industry in which your organization operates? And why?

What trends do you see nationally and internationally related to competition?

It is, of course, impossible to be definitive about all trends in competition. However, with the collapse of communism in eastern Europe, there has been a significant move away from monopolies to free market economies. Government initiative in the UK has also sought to reduce or abolish state control, through, for example, the privatization of the utility industries and the introduction of fundholding general medical practices and health trusts.

Nevertheless, this swing in the direction of free markets has not resulted in much in the way of perfect competition. On the contrary, as investment needs and development costs have risen, the trend has been towards growing members of oligopolies. In fact, there has been serious concern that, for example, as privatized water and electricity companies have been sold off, ownership has become concentrated among a small number of firms, largely overseas.

In their best-known justification of free market economies Milton and Rose Friedman (1979) argued for a major reduction in government intervention as follows:

Our society is what we make it. We can shape our institutions. Physical and human characteristics limit the alternatives available to us. But none prevents us, if we will, from building a society that relies primarily on voluntary co-operation to organise both economic and other activity, a society that preserves and expands human freedom, that keeps government in its place, keeping it our servant and not letting it become our master.

Without doubt, the trends we have described have involved a significant reduction in government control. The extent to which that has brought with it an increase in freedom of choice is less clear-cut.

ACTIVITY 20

Has your business experienced a reduction or an increase in government control?

What have the results been?

Have they been to the benefit of:

- your organization?

- your customers?

The saturated market and limited scope for differentiation

As we mentioned earlier, there are few if any markets left in which customer needs go wholly unsatisfied. The marketplace has been described as:

- 'too many suppliers chasing too few customers'
- 'a graveyard of failed initiatives'
- 'where success depends on money, muscle and stamina'

More positively, this saturated market has become one that demands increasing attention to the needs of the customer, where the only possibility of marketing success depends on a painstaking focus on small ways of improving the elements of the marketing mix.

Most organizations are responding to this challenge by attempting to make customer-orientation central to their operations. Relevant initiatives include:

- quality focus, including TQM, Quality Circles, ISO9000 and ISO9001
- restructuring the organization to encourage greater innovation through smaller, self-managed workgroups
- increased delegation of responsibility for planning and implementing change and improvement
- tighter market segmentation to allow the identification of unexploited niches
- shorter lead times for new product development and product improvement
- improved marketing information
- new and more sophisticated approaches to customer research
- quicker decisions to drop declining or unprofitable ranges
- constant efforts to find and exploit new markets, often overseas
- heavy investment in upgrading production resources and processes

Hugh Davidson (1987) encapsulates these approaches in a checklist he calls 'criteria for rating a business on offensive attitudes'. His checklist appears in Activity 21.

ACTIVITY 21   A6.2

Take some photocopies, then use the checklist to rate both your own organization and those of some of your major competitors.

	Maximum score	Your score
Clear, realistic and motivating vision of the future, understood and accepted by most employees	15	
A strong commitment to providing superior value to customers, backed by low-cost operation	20	
Strong emphasis on innovation throughout the business, both daily build and 'big bang' in the right balance for the industry. Stress on technology, support, recognition and reward for successful innovators. Structure where innovation can flourish	15	
Ability to achieve short-term results, but strong focus on long-term objectives	15	
Commitment to continued investment in all assets, such as brands, people, new products and equipment, even when faced by strong short-term pressures	15	
Overall focus on attacking competition, but at carefully chosen times and places	15	
Fast, good quality response to new opportunities or competitive threats	10	
TOTAL	100	

Now answer the following questions in Activity 22.

ACTIVITY 22   A6.2

How did you compare overall with your competitors?

What are the principal strengths you identified?

How might your organization exploit them?

What weaknesses did you identify?

What action is needed to address them?

Summary

In this section we have examined the competitive environment of the organization.

The key areas of consideration have been:

■ the bases on which an organization can compete
■ national, international trends and globalization
■ where to compete and where to collaborate
■ scope for organizations to differentiate products and services

Section 4
Responsible to whom?

Changing views of stakeholders

In Section 1 of this workbook, we asked you to consider how your organization defines its stakeholders. We return to that theme now.

Textbook definitions of stakeholders range from the very narrow to the very broad. F.A. Hayek (1969) stated:

There are four groups on whose behalf it might be claimed that the corporations ought to be run in their interest: management, labor, stockholders and 'the public' at large. So far as management is concerned, we can dismiss it briefly with the observation that, though it is perhaps a danger to be guarded against, nobody would probably seriously contend that it is desirable that corporations should be run primarily on their interest.

The interest of 'labor' demands only a little longer consideration. As soon as it is made clear that it is not a question of the interest of workers in general but of the special interest of the employers of a particular corporation, it is fairly obvious that it would not be in the interest of 'society' or even of labor in general that the corporation should be run mainly for the benefit of any particular closed group of people employed by it ...

There remains, then, as possible claimants for the position of the dominating interest in whose service the individual corporation ought to be conducted, the owners of the equity and the public at large ... I will briefly consider the consequences which would follow if it were to become the accepted view that the managements of corporations are entitled to spend corporate funds on what they regard as socially desirable purposes. The range of such purposes which might come to be regarded as legitimate objects of corporate expenditure is very wide; political, charitable, educational and in fact everything which can be brought under the vague and almost meaningless term social... So long as the management is supposed to serve the interest of the stockholders, it is reasonable to leave the control of its action to the stockholders. But if the management is supposed to serve wider public interests, it becomes merely a logical consequence of this conception that the appointed representatives of the public interest should control the management.

Having argued against the suggestion that corporations exist to serve management, employees or the public at large, Hayek goes on to propose changes in the law that would make corporations more directly accountable to individual stockholders. He concludes his argument as follows:

The chief merit of these changes would seem to be that they would tie management much more effectively than is now the case to the single task of employing the capital of their stockholders in the most profitable manner and would deprive management of the power of using it in the service of some 'public interest'. The present tendency not only to allow but to encourage such use of corporate resources appears to me as dangerous in its short-run as in its long-run consequences.

ACTIVITY 23

What is your response to Hayek's arguments?

Ignores environment,

FEEDBACK

You may well have felt some sympathy for the argument. After all, since stockholders are the owners of the business, it is surely right that the primary focus of the business should be to use the resources they provide in order to maximize the benefit they receive.

Nevertheless, Hayek's argument runs counter to the view prevailing among most writers on the responsibilities of the organization. Here are just some examples of the opposing view:

Stakeholders to whom the board is accountable include the shareholders, customers, suppliers, employees, the government and the general public. The emphasis and stakeholder priorities vary by country of incorporation and operation:

- *In the UK and US, many directors are reluctant to be 'distracted' by accountabilities other than to shareholders.*
- *In many EC member states, the interests of other stakeholders such as 'social partners' assume a higher priority, while a Japanese board may give greater attention to the pursuit of the business philosophy of the company. (Colin Coulson-Thomas, 1993)*

Organisations have readily recognised the legitimate constraints placed upon them by the stakeholder concept but they have been less ready to recognise that the old patriarchal ideas of property are dying, if not dead, and will be replaced by the notion of community. (Charles Handy, 1985)

The time is now for corporations to accept the notion of participatory democracy as a model for consumer-relations policy. Remember the key question in participatory democracy: are the people who are being affected by a decision part of the process of arriving at that decision? (John Naisbitt, 1984)

The best people are recognised as readily outside the company as within it. The best people involve themselves in their communities and you will find them playing a role disproportionate to their total numbers in such fields as education, the arts, local government and so on. (John Harvey-Jones, 1989)

It is worth noting, of course, that all the authors we have quoted so far are referring directly or indirectly to commercial, profit-making organizations, where the issue of ownership is clearly defined. Consequently, it is relatively easy to distinguish between the company's responsibility to its owners and that to the wider community (suppliers, customers, employees, the general public).

When we consider other organizations – charities, schools, hospitals, for example – the distinctions become less clear-cut and the issue of accountability more complicated.

ACTIVITY 24

Think of a non profit-making organization you know reasonably well.

List all the groups to whom you believe it should hold itself accountable:

Building on the evidence we have presented so far, we believe it is right to work on the assumption that stakeholders in an organization should be defined as broadly as possible. For an organization, that will include employees, suppliers and customers – whether those are the people who buy goods and services from commercial concerns, pupils in schools, patients in hospitals or those who benefit from charities. Equally, any organization has an impact on its local community – as a source of employment (a positive impact) or as a source of noise, congestion and pollution (a negative impact).

The management standards to which we are working broadens this definition still further, by listing the following:

Contractual stakeholders

- shareholders
- employees/voluntary workers
- members
- customers/clients
- suppliers
- lenders

Other stakeholders

- government
- regulators
- electorate
- public
- pressure groups
- media

We will now move on to relate this broad definition to your own organization.

Who are your stakeholders?

Later in this section, we shall be asking you to consider the extent to which your organization's stakeholders are supporting or opposing the achievement of the organization's objectives and how you can increase support and reduce or eliminate opposition. It will not be possible to do this on a broadbrush basis. Instead, you will need to carry out a fairly detailed analysis.

ACTIVITY 25   A6.3

Consider your organization's stakeholders under the headings listed and see if you can summarize their attitudes to your organization. Be as specific as you can.

Contractual stakeholders

Shareholders

Who are they? (Any corporate investors?)

DfEE, colleges & other institutions Ministers.

What are their attitudes?

We do what they say, minimising operational problems

Employees/voluntary workers

Who are they? (Categories, union representation?)

Our staff

What are their attitudes?

Variable

Members (if you are, for example, a professional institution)

Who are they?

Colleges?

What are their attitudes?

Customers/clients

Who are they? (Retail/trade/other. Any major accounts?)

Colleges? & other institutions

What are their attitudes?

Necessary evil? — not always.

Suppliers

Who are they? (Local/national. Any major suppliers?)

What are their attitudes?

Lenders

Who are they? (Banks? Other?)

What are their attitudes?

Other stakeholders

Government

Who are they? (Local/national. Political persuasion?)

What are their attitudes?

Regulators

Who are they? (What power do they have?)

What are their attitudes?

Electorate
Who are they? (What power/influence do they have?)

What are their attitudes?

Public
Who are they? (What relationship/interdependence do you have with them?
Any specific categories?)

What are their attitudes?

Pressure groups
Who are they? (e.g. environmental? consumerist?)

What are their attitudes?

Media
Who are they? (Local/national? What influence do they have?)

What are their attitudes?

You should now have a general picture of the level of support for or opposition to the achievement of your organization's objectives. We will now move on to relate that picture specifically to your organization's objectives.

Stakeholders: helping or hindering

Earlier in this section, you may have been thinking that holding your organization accountable to the wide range of stakeholders we listed does no more than complicate organizational life for no reason other than to satisfy a vague social obligation.

In fact, as you probably recognized, the reason is far more compelling. All the groups we mentioned have the potential to help or hinder the success of your organization. There are several historical examples of this happening.

CASE STUDY

Marks and Spencer's national reputation as a retailer of high quality merchandise with enlightened employment practices means it is able to select from the best graduates for its management trainee scheme.

The **Ralph Nader** consumerist organization in the USA has been instrumental in influencing public opinion away from traditional 'gas guzzler' cars to more economical – mainly imported – models.

Fiat Motor Company in the UK found its reputation as a slow payer made it difficult to gain and keep suppliers.

Saatchi and Saatchi, the international advertising agency, suffered from critical media coverage of its support for the Conservative Party in the UK.

Consequently, the process of 'winning friends and influencing people' is fundamental to the successful operation of your organization. The following simple case study provides an example of the sort of things we mean.

CASE STUDY

The Alpha Light Engineering Company manufactures components for a range of consumer durables. It currently operates from a single factory on an industrial estate in the south of England.

Faced with increasing demand for its products, it wishes to open a second factory on a greenfield site in the north.

ACTIVITY 26

Who among Alpha's stakeholders will need to support this initiative?

Shareholders - for the money
Employees - to relocate
New community - to provide site & staff.
Customers - to continue to buy.

FEEDBACK

We deliberately kept the details of the case study to a minimum. As a result, you may have been surprised by the length of the list of stakeholders you came up with! Compare it with ours.

Contractual stakeholders

- *Shareholders*: unless Alpha is able to fund the new factory wholly from reserves, it may well need to offer, for example, a rights issue.
- *Employees*: operatives will probably be recruited locally, but it is likely that some more senior staff will be asked to transfer.
- *Customers*: demand for the product is growing, but will customers – particularly those in the south – be prepared to source components from the new location?
- *Suppliers*: do existing raw material suppliers have enough confidence in Alpha to want to supply the new factory?
- *Lenders*: bank borrowing may be an alternative to new shareholder funding

Other stakeholders

- *Government*: will local government see the new factory as a welcome resource of employment and trade, or as a noisy and disruptive incursion into open countryside? Will national government provide development grants and employment subsidies?
- *Electorate*: if there is a local election looming, will the new factory be an issue?
- *Public*: will local people want to work for Alpha? Will they accept or oppose the loss of open land and the resultant disruption?
- *Pressure groups*: how will environmental groups respond to the new building and the possible need for new road access?
- *Media*: this is unlikely to warrant national coverage, but how will the local press react?

We will now get you to apply the same thinking process to your own organization's future strategy.

ACTIVITY 27

Start by listing up to four major initiatives from your organization's current strategic plan. These may be external initiatives – marketing, product development, expansion, for example. Or internal initiatives – changes to structure, operating practices, changes of responsibility. Or ideally, a combination of both. Summarize them below:

Initiative 1

Initiative 2

Initiative 3

Initiative 4

Next, list the stakeholders whose support you will need in order to facilitate the success of each initiative, the nature of that support and the current likelihood of your organization receiving it?

Initiative 1

Stakeholders	Support needed	Current likelihood

Initiative 2

Stakeholders	Support needed	Current likelihood

Initiative 3

Stakeholders	Support needed	Current likelihood

Initiative 4

Stakeholders	Support needed	Current likelihood

We can now build on Activity 27 by considering the actions you may be able to take to influence stakeholders in your favour. In general, the principles and techniques we suggest will be obvious and straightforward. For all that, they are often overlooked or ignored!

Influencing contractual stakeholders

SHAREHOLDERS

For many organizations, their only contact with shareholders takes place through the publication of half-yearly or interim results, the annual report and the shareholder's AGM. Even then, a large number of boards take the view that the management of the business is their affair and that information given to shareholders should be kept to the legal minimum. Is it surprising if shareholders begin to lose confidence, when they know little about what is happening in the business or the reasons for it?

CASE STUDY

A notable exception to this approach is Eurotunnel. Faced with a succession of financial and operational crises, the company has taken care to keep both its individual and corporate shareholders fully informed about the progress and success of its initiatives. Some of the published information has made uncomfortable reading, but it can be argued that this process of regular and frequent communication has gone some way to maintaining a degree of confidence and consequent shareholder loyalty.

Other organizations, while limiting themselves to the publication of interim and annual results, take care to ensure that the information presented in them goes well beyond the legal minimum. It is, of course, tempting to see a glossy annual report as no more than an attempt to disguise poor performance with attractive visuals and optimistic text. However, experience of reading such reports makes it reasonably easy to spot inconsistencies and anomalies, particularly when the text is compared with, for example the Profit and Loss Account or the Balance Sheet.

In summary, we can say that gaining the support of shareholders depends on, as a minimum, a regular flow of up-to-date, accurate and comprehensive information. If you want to go further, promote regular involvement of your institutional investors in strategic decision making. Too often, a seat on the Board is required before funding is made available. As a result, involvement in decision making is resented as unjustified interference. On the contrary, this kind of involvement often results in a much-needed new perspective.

EMPLOYEES

The management literature is full of suggestions for gaining the support and commitment of employees.

ACTIVITY 28

What methods can you think of for gaining the support and commitment of employees?

Which of them have you seen in action?

FEEDBACK

The following list may not be comprehensive but it does highlight some of the best-known techniques for gaining the support and commitment of employees.

Communication with employees

■ cascade or team briefings
■ 'walking the job'
■ on-line video links
■ regular open forums
■ newsletters

Employee involvement in decision making

■ employee directors
■ management union partnerships
■ quality circles
■ 'bottom-up, top-down' strategy planning

All of the above approaches start from the position that employee support is greatest when employees know about their organization – the good news, the bad news where performance is good and where it is not – and are involved in the decisions that concern them. That position is fundamentally opposed to the old hierarchical dictum that 'managers are there to give instructions and employees are there to obey them'.

Unsurprising though this may seem, the history of labour unrest and poor employee relations is littered with the resentment of people whose main complaints are that they 'weren't informed' or 'weren't consulted'. As with the most basic approach to motivation, gaining employee support comes from treating people as intelligent, capable human beings.

CUSTOMERS/CLIENTS

Rosabeth Moss Kanter (1989) explains:

There have always been strategic advantages to staying close to customers. Good customer relationships reverberate not only in current sales but also in future effectiveness and growth. Satisfied customers are the single best source of new business. Timely knowledge of changing customer requirements makes it possible to guide production more efficiently, reducing waste, inventory costs and returns. And experience shows that customers are also one of the major founts of ideas for innovation. In some industries, as much as 80% of all important industrial innovations have originated with users. These are among the reasons that innovation conscious high technology companies go beyond emphasising customer service to create more formal ties: user councils, inviting customers to consult on R&D projects, joint promotions and the ultimate partnership step, joint development projects.

The principle does not apply simply to high technology companies either. In the chapter headed 'Close to the customer' from *In Search of Excellence*, Peters and Waterman (1982) refer to the importance of 'service obsession', 'quality obsession' and 'listening to the user' for companies as different as Walt Disney Productions, Caterpillar Tractor, McDonald's, Ogilvy and Mather, Bloomingdale's and Boeing, to name just a few.

Gaining customer support involves action to find out what they need, meeting and exceeding those expectations before, during and particularly after the sale, and, perhaps above all, involving and consulting with customers.

SUPPLIERS

CASE STUDY

Marks and Spencer is probably the best-known British example of a close relationship between purchaser and supplier.

Manufacturers new to Marks and Spencer are given strict guidance on plant layout, quality control, production and packaging methods. Established manufacturers are visited regularly to ensure that quality is being maintained and systems followed. In its heyday, this close relationship meant that suppliers could rely on the retailer for the success and profitability of their business.

The pressure on retail margins has tended to bring patriarchal relationships into disrepute by requiring suppliers to operate on very narrow profits, while making them highly vulnerable to changes in fashion.

Rosabeth Moss Kanter (1989) describes a more modern version of this close relationship, which offers similar benefits:

Facing imperatives to cut costs and improve quality, leading American companies are creating closer relationships with their suppliers. 'Outsourcing' is one way American high-tech firms are addressing productivity issues — buying more instead of making it in-house; 41 per cent of the firms in a 1988 American Electronics Association survey planned to increase the value of the product outsourced, while only 18 per cent intended to decrease it. But those same firms saw quality as their number one competitive factor. To ensure quality while buying from outside firms calls for a redefinition of the vendor relationship. Arm's length relationships do not produce the motivation for suppliers to invest in technology to improve quality or manage the technology of just-in-time inventory.

Thus, leading companies are starting to treat suppliers as their 'partners'. John Marshall, vice-president of TRW Safety Systems Division told George Lodge about this change at TRW's automotive divisions.

> *'In the past we sought bids from a number of suppliers and price was the principal issue. Now we want flexible relationships with a few suppliers, and we want our suppliers to help us in a variety of ways. We want better quality. We want them to help us reduce our inventories. We want their help and ideas about how we can improve the final products. It is not unusual these days for two or three engineers from our suppliers to be working in our plants for a while. We network through computers. I might call one of our suppliers and urge them — if not help them — to find a plant near us.'*

In addition to making possible joint investments in technology and compatible systems *that improve quality and reduce waste, supplier input into product design can generate innovation by taking advantage of the suppliers' expertise in the potential of their technologies. At the same time, helping suppliers manage better also has pay-offs. Polaroid save $27 million over two years by helping vendors to improve their cost structure. To do this required knowing the suppliers' businesses well and showing them ways to operate more efficiently.*

A familiar theme is emerging once again. The key to gaining supplier support is to eliminate the old adversarial relationship and to adopt a co-operative, joint venture style of operation.

LENDERS

There is not a lot left to say under this final heading in our list of contractual stakeholders. The principles to which we have already referred – those of openness, involvement and regular consultation apply as much to lenders as they do to other contractual stakeholders.

ACTIVITY 29   A6.3

We now return to Activity 27. Look back to your list of strategic initiatives and the stakeholders whose support you identified as necessary to their success. Which of them were contractual stakeholders? And, based on what you have read so far, what action might you now take to gain their support?

Initiative 1

Contractual stakeholders	Action to gain support

Initiative 2

Contractual stakeholders	Action to gain support

Initiative 3

Contractual stakeholders	Action to gain support

Initiative 4

Contractual stakeholders	Action to gain support

Influencing other stakeholders

GOVERNMENT

There has been considerable media coverage recently of abuses of the lobbying process, by which organizations have traditionally sought the support of national government. However, it should be stressed that there have been abuses of a process that is both traditional and well established – and unlikely to disappear.

It is not controversial to assert that, under a system of open government, individuals and organizations have the right to put their case to both local and national elected representatives. Without descending to the need for bribery and corrupt practices, there are numerous opportunities for organizations to argue for support – through select committees, commissions of enquiry, to individual representatives.

As in most other situations, a convincing argument will be one that has been properly researched, is based on fact, offers relevant benefits and is well presented. This may be verbally, in a written submission or visually. Of course, it will not be possible to make a convincing argument if none exists. Consequently, it is important to ensure that there is some merit in the case you are presenting!

REGULATORS

Similar principles apply if your organization or industry is subject to inspection by a statutory regulator. You will need to make sure that the data and information you submit answer the regulator's questions, are justified and accurate.

And, if, for example, you are arguing against a price freeze or in favour of greater freedom, you will need a set of arguments that offer real benefits to support your case.

ELECTORATE

As with lobbying government, the question of influencing the electorate takes us back into potentially murky waters. Nevertheless, the practice of funding political parties that are broadly sympathetic to the aims of your organization is well established and there are opportunities to contribute to the policies they advocate through forums such as the CBI, TUC and professional bodies.

PUBLIC

We have already quoted John Harvey-Jones on the importance of involving people from your organization in community activities. The list of opportunities here is almost limitless:

- school and university governing bodies
- hospital trusts
- local and national charities
- voluntary organizations
- speaking to professional institutes

In fact, the only problems are likely to be ensuring that those people who represent you are effective ambassadors for the organization – and that they still have enough time to do the jobs you pay them for!

Nevertheless, it is important that, for example, speakers are trained to present well, advisors know their subjects and that, overall, your representatives give a favourable impression of the organization.

The question of which bodies to support is largely a marketing issue. It is a matter of deciding which segments of the total population you most want to influence and targeting those bodies where your chosen segments are best represented.

Beyond that, influencing the public in your favour depends largely on common sense.

- Do members of your staff praise or criticize the organization to outsiders?
- Are your premises attractive or unsightly?
- Are your delivery drivers polite or aggressive on the road?

It is a salutary lesson to stand back and view all aspects of your organization through the eyes of the public and ask yourself what impression they convey.

PRESSURE GROUPS

The starting point for influencing pressure groups is understanding their membership, their priorities and objectives. Even a small group, apparently with a single objective – to oppose the building of a new road, for example – is likely to be made up of people with a range of different motivations.

As a result, it may well be possible to gain the support of such a group by offering a range of small concessions, each of which will satisfy one of the subsets of the group.

Alternatively, if one of your strategic initiatives is likely to rouse the opposition of a pressure group, it may be because they do not know the benefits the initiative will bring. As we pointed out earlier, you will find it helpful to communicate your case in such a way that it addresses their concerns by offering enough advantages to outweigh the drawbacks they foresee. The important point is to avoid making assumptions about the motivation and objectives of the group. Understanding is all-important.

MEDIA

Relations with the media is a big enough subject to warrant a book to itself! However, there are some key issues that are essential to the process of gaining favourable editorial coverage for your organization.

First, while the media are always hungry for news, it has to be real news – at least as far as the national media are concerned. Journalists' wastebaskets are constantly filled with press releases dealing with events that are of major relevance to the organization they concern, but of no interest at all to the public. Local media, by contrast, are happy to publish less newsworthy items, provided they have a genuine local connection.

Second, media editors are far more likely to use a press release if they do not have to rewrite it. There is an art to writing media copy in such a way that it is punchy, can be lifted straight onto the page and makes sense even if one or more paragraphs are cut out to make it fit.

Third, journalists want to be leaders rather than followers. An item featured in one paper yesterday will not be included in a different paper today. It is therefore important to make a careful choice of your target publications, selecting those which reflect the sort of image you want to convey to your organization.

Finally, personal contacts within the media are crucial. It is worth spending time and effort gaining a media reputation as an organization with something meaningful and authoritative to say on issues related to your industry. Some larger organizations go as far as preparing statements on topics of current interest, even if they are asked for only rarely. At a national level, the media will have editors responsible for industry matters, financial matters and so on. They are worth identifying and cultivating.

ACTIVITY 30   A6.3

Look back to the stakeholders you identified in Activity 27 who do not have a contractual relationship with your organization. Use Section 4.5 to prompt your thoughts on how you might gain their support for your initiatives.

Initiative 1

Other stakeholders	Action to gain support

Initiative 2

Other stakeholders	Action to gain support

Initiative 3

Other stakeholders	Action to gain support

Initiative 4

Other stakeholders	Action to gain support

Summary

In this section we have examined the importance of stakeholders to organizations.

Specifically we have covered:

- who are, and who are not stakeholders
- the difference between types of stakeholders
- the needs of stakeholders
- aligning stakeholders' needs with the strategy of the organization
- influencing stakeholder groups

Section 5   'If you're not in business for fun or profit, what the hell are you doing here?'

The importance of a vision

The title of this section is taken from the front cover of Robert Townsend's *Up the Organisation* (1971). In it, the former chairman of Avis Rent-a-Car sets out his often iconoclastic views on how to run a business.

We believe the challenge implicit in Townsend's question is crucial because it raises some fundamental issues about the purpose and direction of an organization and, equally importantly, about people's commitment to it.

ACTIVITY 31

Think about a cross-section of people in your organization. Make sure they come from a variety of levels – managers, supervisors, operatives, clerical staff, members of the sales force. Then try to answer the following questions related to them.

Do your people have a clear idea of what the organization exists to achieve?

Yes

If so, how would they express that purpose?

To manage public funds for FE.

Are people excited by it?

Doubt it.

Does that statement of purpose accurately reflect how the organization actually operates?

We have called an organization's overriding reason for existence a 'statement of purpose'. In the literature of strategic management, you will see it described alternatively as:

- a mission or mission statement
- a vision or vision statement
- a business aim

Townsend (1971) refers to it as an organization's objective. This is an unusual use of the term, because objectives normally refer to a set of measurable, quantified targets that an organization seeks to achieve in a given period of time.

Nevertheless, when Townsend talks about objectives, it is clear that he is describing the organization's overriding purpose or direction. Here is what he has to say about Avis's objective:

One of the important functions of a leader is to make the organisation concentrate on its objectives. In the case of Avis, it took us six months to define one objective – which turned out to be: 'We want to become the fastest-growing company with the highest profit margins in the business of renting and leasing vehicles without drivers'.

That objective was simple enough so that we didn't have to write it down. We could put it in every speech and talk about it wherever we went. ...

It also included a definition of our business 'renting and leasing vehicles without drivers'. This let us put the blinders on ourselves and stop considering the acquisition of related businesses like motels, hotels, airlines and travel agencies. It also showed us that we had to get rid of some limousine and sightseeing companies that we already owned. Once these objectives were agreed on, the leader must be merciless on himself and on his people. If an idea that pops into his head or out of their mouths is outside the objective of the company, he kills it without trial. ...

It isn't easy to concentrate. I used to keep a sign by my desk where I couldn't miss it if I was on the telephone .... or in a meeting in my office. 'Is what I'm doing or about to do getting us closer to our objective?

Read through that extract again, then answer the questions in Activity 32.

ACTIVITY 32

Does your organization have a vision statement that gives it a clear focus and direction?

Probably not.

If so, what is it?

How clearly is it communicated, both inside and outside the organization?

Do members of the organization use it as a basis for decision making?

Don't think so

We hope that, by now, you are beginning to see both the importance and the value of a vision for the organization. In particular, we hope you have recognized that a vision statement

But PBFC's direction is determined

■ sets a challenging purpose to aim for
■ requires senior management to think clearly about the direction of the organization
■ provides a definition, not only of what the organization is but also of what it is not
■ gives everyone the chance to identify with the organization as a whole, not just with their small part of it
■ takes away the need for detailed rules and instructions by providing an overriding reason for the organization's existence

And, last but not least, a vision statement has the potential to give people pride in the value of their organization and the contribution they make to its success. Notice we referred to 'potential' in that last statement. We will explore that theme further now.

Strategic vision versus motivating vision

Ansoff (1965), the guru of strategic planning, wrote:

We shall develop in this and the following chapter a system of objectives which is based on the following premises.

1 *The firm has both (a) 'economic' objectives aimed at optimizing the efficiency of its total resource-conversion process and (b) 'social' or non-economic objectives, which are the result of interaction among individual objectives of the firm's participants.*

2 *In most firms the economic objectives exert the primary influence on the firm's behaviour and form the main body of explicit goals used by management for guidance and control of the firm.*

3 *The central purpose of the firm is to maximize long-term return on resources employed within the firm.*

4 *The social objectives exert a secondary modifying and constraining influence on management behaviour.*

5 *In addition to proper objectives two related types of influence are exerted on management behaviour, responsibilities and constraints.*

Ansoff then goes on to propose a formal planning system that, using subsidiary objectives and across a range of time-scales, seeks to achieve the best possible return on investment for the firm.

For many organizations, this hierarchical and quantitative approach is still the norm. Indeed, most organizations that follow a structural planning process tend to adopt it. After all, it is self-evident that individuals and departments need goals to aim for which will contribute to the overall success of the organization. And the most convenient form of those goals to take is based on numbers – profit, return, productivity and so on. Indeed, the whole philosophy of management control based on management by objectives assumes that the effectiveness of an organization can be measured by numbers.

However, current management literature has raised several questions about the validity of this mainly quantified approach.

ACTIVITY 33

What doubts do you have personally about a mainly numerical approach to strategic planning?

FEEDBACK

You may have mentioned any or all of the following:

- the future unpredictability of the environment
- people may raise objections
- the need for continuity

THE FUTURE UNPREDICTABILITY OF THE ENVIRONMENT

Ansoff acknowledges this objection and deals with it by building-in what he calls a 'flexibility objective'. He explains this as follows:

.... probable trends can be upset by unforeseeable events which may have relatively low probability of occurrence, but whose impact on profitability of the opportunity and of the firm as a whole would be major. The impact may be negative with catastrophic consequences, or positive (the word 'breakthrough' is often used to describe it), opening wide vistas to the firm.

Although some catastrophes can be anticipated, a firm which tries to predict revolutions and inventions is undertaking a highly unproductive job. On the other hand, a firm can effectively buy itself insurance against catastrophes and put itself in the way of potential discoveries. This can be done by adding another major objective to the firm's mother list – flexibility objective. Flexibility can be measured by two proxy objectives: external flexibility achieved through a diversified pattern of product-market investments and internal flexibility through liquidity of resources.

Notice, however, two key factors in Ansoff's approach to unpredictability. The first is the assumption that unforeseeable events are relatively unlikely and the second is the recommendation that their impact can be minimized by adopting measures that are themselves quantifiable. In today's fast-changing business environment, neither assertion is justifiable.

WHAT ABOUT THE PEOPLE?

More recent literature has taken a significantly different view. Peters and Waterman's (1982) is typical. Although the book has been criticized for an unfortunate choice of 'excellent' companies, it has nevertheless introduced a strategic philosophy very much at odds with the strict formality of earlier approaches, by emphasizing the importance of people in the planning process.

In the chapter headed 'Man Waiting for Motivation', the authors state:

The central problem with the rationalist view of organising people is that people are not very rational. To fit Taylor's old model, or today's organisational charts, man is simply designed wrong (or, of course, vice versa, according to our argument here). In fact, if our understanding of the current state of psychology is even close to correct, man is the ultimate study in conflict and paradox. It seems to us that to understand why the excellent companies are so effective in engendering both commitment and regular innovation from tens of thousands or even hundreds of thousands of people, we have to take into account the way they deal with the following introductions that are built into human nature:

1   All of us are self-centred, suckers for a bit of praise and generally like to think of ourselves as winners. But the fact of the matter is that our talents are distributed normally – none of us is really as good as he or she would like to think, but rubbing our noses daily in that reality doesn't do us a bit of good.

2   Our imaginative, symbolic right brain is at least as important as our rational deductive left. We reason by stories at least as often as with good data. 'Does it feel right?' counts for more than 'Does it add up?' or 'Can I prove it?'

3   As information processors, we are simultaneously flawed and wonderful. On the one hand, we can hold little explicitly in mind, at most a half dozen or so facts at one time. Hence there should be an enormous pressure on managements – of complex organisations especially – to keep things very simple indeed. On the other hand, our unconscious mind is powerful, accumulating a vast storehouse of patterns, if we let it. Experience is an excellent teacher; yet most businessmen seem to undervalue it in the special sense we will describe.

4   We are creatures of our environment, very sensitive and responsive to external rewards and punishments. We are also strongly driven from within, self-motivated.

5   We act as if express beliefs are important, yet action speaks louder than words. One cannot, it turns out, fool any of the people any of the time. They watch for patterns in our most minute actions, and are wise enough to distrust words that in any way mismatch our deeds.

6   We desperately need meaning in our lives and will sacrifice a great deal to institutions that will provide meaning for us. We simultaneously need independence, to feel as though we are in charge of our destinies and to have the ability to stick out.

Tom Peters (1988) summarizes these points further:

Following and administering rules might have been dandy in the placid environment of yesteryear. Not today. Managers must create new worlds. And then destroy them; and then create anew. Such brave acts of creation must begin with a vision that not only inspires, ennobles, empowers and challenges, but at the same time provokes confidence enough, in the midst of a perpetual competitive hurricane, to encourage people to take the day-to-day risks involved in testing and adapting and extending the vision.

THE NEED FOR CONTINUITY

Objectives, by definition, are there to be achieved. Typically set for delivery in six or twelve months, objectives, once achieved, are replaced by new objectives. As we shall see in Section 6, objectives need to be realistic, stretching but achievable. If they meet those criteria, they are likely to be sources of short-term motivation and personal satisfaction when they have been achieved. What they will not do, however, is give people that sense of belonging to a secure, dependable organization.

That is where the vision and values of the organization come in. The vision or mission statement should be broad, general and very long term. As Gordon Oliver (1986) points out:

At the highest level the organization's purpose is defined in its mission. This gives very broad guidelines about what the organization wants to become in the future.

Michael Armstrong (1990) links mission and values as follows:

The mission of an organisation expresses its sense of purpose – the business the enterprise is in and the broad direction in which it is going ....

A value system expresses basic beliefs in the behaviour which is believed to be good for an organisation and in what the organisation considers to be important. It is expressed in a value statement.

The purpose of a value system is to help to develop a value-drive and committed organisation which conducts its business successfully by reference to shared beliefs and an understanding of what is best for the enterprise. Value statements are therefore an integral part of strategic planning as means of guiding the direction of effort in the longer term.

Value statements are closely associated with mission statements and like them can be used as levers for change, getting people to act differently in ways which will support the attainment of the organisation's objections.

A value statement defines core values in such areas as:

- *care and consideration for people*
- *care for customers*

- *competitiveness*
- *enterprise*
- *excellence*
- *flexibility*
- *growth as a major objective*
- *innovation*
- *market/customer orientation*
- *performance orientation*
- *productivity*
- *quality*
- *teamwork*

Thomas J. Watson Junior, son of the founder of IBM and later his successor as chief executive, distilled the company's values into just three instructions:

- give full consideration to the individual employee
- spend a lot of time making customers happy
- go the last mile to do things right

In summary then, we suggest that an organization's vision statement should:

- be short enough to be memorable
- be fully communicated and understood throughout the organization
- provide focus and direction
- engender a sense of purpose, pride and commitment
- enable people to take their own decisions with the confidence that they know what is right for the organization

ACTIVITY 34

Use the above criteria to evaluate the vision statement of your organization.

Is it:
Memorable?

If not, how would you change it?

Communicated and understood?

If not, what could be done about it?

Does it:
Provide focus and direction?

If not, how would you change it?

Engender pride and commitment?

If not, how would you change it?

Support decision making?

If not, what could be done about it?

Contrary to the title with which we started, we have argued that there is no contradiction between a strategic vision and a motivating vision. The reality is that an effective strategic vision must motivate and inspire as well as provide guidance and direction. As we shall see in Section 6, it is only when the vision is translated into objectives (in Ansoff's meaning of the term) that the importance of motivation becomes subsumed into the need for measurable goals.

Developing a mission statement

The vision or mission statement provides an answer to the question:

'What business are we (or should we be) in?'

Theodore Levitt (1975) argued that firms should define their businesses very broadly. 'The energy business' not 'the oil business', 'the transport business' not 'the railroad business', 'the entertainment business' not 'the movie business'. The point he was making was that firms should focus on the current and future needs of customers, rather than on their own expertise or traditions.

However, as R. L. Willsmer (1979) pointed out:

The problem with extending the business horizon is how far do you go? If a newspaper is part of the communication business, its potential competition is enormous. 'Communication' can encompass a whole range of audio, visual, audio-visual, transitory, permanent and semi-permanent media, sandwich boards and megaphones. The danger with such descriptive definitions is that they are too global, too nearly all-embracing.

There are many examples of firms falling into that trap. WH Smith saw itself in the 1980s as a highly capable retailer and expanded from its high street books, news and stationery operations into confectionery, craft materials and travel agencies. All lost money. The company took a long time to realize that its strengths and experience were far more limited than they had at first assumed. Lloyds Bank diversified into the 'Black Horse' chain of estate agents, then discovered they lacked the necessary expertise to survive as the market contracted. They withdrew.

The consequent message, which takes us back to the first section of this workbook, is that a mission statement should reflect not only the needs of customers in the marketplace, but also the expertise and experience of the organization. As Peters and Waterman (1982) point out:

It is a simple fact that most acquisitions go awry. Not only are the synergies to which so many executives pay lip service seldom realised; more often than not the result is catastrophic. Frequently the executives of the acquired companies leave. ... More important, acquisitions, even little ones, suck up an inordinate amount of top management's time, time taken away from the main-line businesses. ... The typical diversification strategy dilutes the guiding qualitative theme – in part because the acquired institution has different shared values, but also because themes, even general themes such as quality, tend to lose meaning when the organization strays far afield. Management loses its 'feel'.

The authors define the guiding principle contained in this chapter of *In Search of Excellence* as:

■ Stick to the Knitting

ACTIVITY 35

What has been your organization's experience of diversification?

Has it been successful?

Does your organization's mission statement take account of customer needs?

Does it take account of experience and expertise?

Does it need changing?

So far, we have stressed the value of a vision or mission statement in terms of corporate direction, motivation and individual decision making. We will now focus on some wider benefits of the strategic planning process, in order to give some more guidance on developing a vision.

The Gower Handbook of Management (1987) spells out the objectives of the planning process as follows:

1 *Improve strategic problem solving within a business and communication between corporate management and business management.*
2 *Build a bridge between strategic thinking and functional operational action.*
3 *Clarify objectives, strategies and action plans throughout different levels of the organization.*
4 *Mobilise potential corporate synergy so that the power of the firm is fully exploited and its resources deployed to optimum advantage in meeting its strategic goals.*
5 *Provide a framework within which managers are motivated to action by having participated in the goal-setting process as well as the formulation of specific strategies and action plans. This provides the basis of a psychological contract and the means for highlighting performance so that desired behaviour can be rewarded and consistent under-achievement eliminated.*

6 Create a mechanism for providing early warning of fundamental environmental changes as well as the tools for developing and implementing appropriate kinds of business and organizational responses.

ACTIVITY 36

What lessons can you draw from that extract about the development of a corporate vision?

FEEDBACK

We thought that the significant points related to developing a vision were:

■ the suggestion that the planning process can improve communication between corporate management and business management
■ the idea of the planning process as a bridge between strategic thinking and operational action
■ planning as a process of clarification through different organization levels
■ motivation through participation in goal setting

Overall, the clear message is that, if corporate strategy is to be a living mechanism, as opposed to 'a document issued once a year that gathers dust on a shelf until next year's version appears', it should involve all levels of people in an organization. And that principle applies above all to the development of a vision.

Tilles (1969) states:

One of the major difficulties in developing a statement of corporate strategy is that in most companies, the attempt to do so coincides with the beginning of a formal planning effort. As a result, all of the complex conceptual and procedural issues related to the corporate future tend to get bound up with the first groping efforts to work out a viable mission and program for the corporate planning activity.

The most common causes of difficulty are the premature establishment of a formal planning department and the separation of the responsibility for the future of the company from the responsibility for managing current operations ....

Strategic planning is not what the planner does, but rather what the management does. If the management finds that it is so deeply involved in the process that it requires some additional assistance, a planning officer may provide this. But to view the planner as synonymous with planning is to assume that a statement of corporate strategy remains a document rather than a creed. ...

The way to get started, then, is to have those who are responsible for the present welfare of the company as well as those who are responsible for its future strategy involved in trying to develop a statement of strategy.

The message is clear. The development of a mission statement needs to involve all those who will be responsible for delivering it. The texts we have quoted refer implicitly or explicitly to the need for line managers to be involved. However, we believe that the current move to autonomous work-groups and flatter structures means that the development of a vision is not just a management responsibility, but that of all members of an organization.

Of course, that makes the process messy. It will require consultation, debate, disagreement and constant revision before the final version is produced. Without the mess, though, the mission statement will be neither accurate nor accepted.

ACTIVITY 37

How was your organization's mission statement developed?

Does it serve its purpose?

Who would you involve in revising it?

Gaining support for the mission statement

As you have worked through this section, you have almost certainly recognized the need for people throughout the organization to 'buy in' to its mission statement. After all, organizations achieve nothing corporately – results come from individuals and teams working together. At the same time, you have probably picked up a range of ideas, either directly or indirectly, concerning ways to gain support for the mission statement.

ACTIVITY 38

How might you gain support for your organization's mission statement :

During its development or revision?

After it has been finalized?

FEEDBACK

The process of developing or revising a mission statement offers almost limitless opportunities to gain support by involving people:

- through buzz groups
- through individual or small group interviews
- through facilitated discussions
- through suggestion schemes
- by publishing and inviting comments on drafts
- by encouraging elected representation
- by involving the union

Gaining support for an existing vision or mission statement is a more complex process, but worth the effort because it depends on ensuring that the organization genuinely lives by its vision and the values which that vision implies. So, for example:

If innovation is central to your organization's vision and values:

- are people encouraged to challenge the status quo?
- are new ideas recognized and rewarded?
- are people encouraged to take risks?
- are failures and mistakes allowed?

Or, if customer satisfaction is a key aspect of the vision:

- are people encouraged to look out for unsatisfied needs?
- do teams treat each other as internal customers?
- does the organization monitor satisfaction levels?
- are the results published?
- are complaints welcomed and dealt with effectively?
- are they analysed to identify inadequate systems?

ACTIVITY 39

Does your organization live its vision?

If not, what could you do about it?

Public or private vision?

Understandably, the full details of an organization's strategy are rarely published. If they are, it is usually many years after the event, as a business school case study. The need for secrecy is obvious – take-over targets, promotional plans, R&D initiatives would all, if made public, give the kind of warning that would doom the strategy to failure.

Corporate vision, though, is a different matter. For a long time, an organization's mission or vision was seen as an inseparable part of its strategy and, consequently, treated with as much secrecy as its growth targets or advertising spend. Nowadays, by contrast, organizations are making increasing efforts to publicize their vision to the outside world. John Harvey-Jones (1988), former chairman of ICI, explains why:

It helps enormously if the external regard for your organisation is high. It needs particularly to be so in the communities in which you operate. Again, in our case, it is an absolute requirement that we should have the support of the localities in which we place our factories. Not everybody wishes to live near a chemical factory. We have to recognise that it is our responsibility to ensure that the natural fears and concerns that people have are allayed. We require also to recruit and motivate the best people and this in turn requires a good reputation, not only for the goods we make and the worthiness of our contribution to society, but also the way in which we do these things, the sort of people we employ and the contributions we make in the area, and whether we are good citizens or not.

Of course, making your vision statement public is not all that is needed to achieve the kind of reputation John Harvey-Jones is describing here. He also talks about community involvement and the contribution individuals can make to education, the arts and local government. Nevertheless, if your organization's vision statement is inspiring enough to motivate your people, there is a good chance that it will have a similar effect on customers, suppliers, potential employees and the community at large – precisely those people, in fact, that we referred to as non-contractual stakeholders in Section 4.

ACTIVITY 40

How public is your organization's vision?

What more could be done to enhance your organization's reputation by making its vision public?

Does your organization live its vision?

If not, what should be done about it?

Summary

In this section we have considered the importance of vision to organization. Specifically, we have covered:

- why vision is important
- the relationship of vision to other strategic concepts
- types of vision statement
- how to develop mission statements
- the relationship to corporate planning
- disseminating and gaining support for mission

Section 6   From where we are to where we want to be

From mission to strategy

In the previous section of this workbook, we examined the need for a vision or mission statement for the organization that would encapsulate its values, philosophy and broad direction. We stressed that the vision should be, to a large extent, timeless and formulated in such a way that it would gain the commitment and support of stakeholders both within and outside the organization.

Valuable though a vision statement is the fact that it is deliberately broad and timeless means that it is of little use in the day-to-day management and control of the organization. For that purpose, we need something more definite – formal statements of objectives, strategies and plans, with quantified targets and time-scales for their achievement. In this section we shall present a structural approach for the translation of a broad, timeless vision into a strategic planning process that will permit an organization's managers to manage effectively.

You may already follow such a process. In that case, this section will provide a convenient checklist against which to assess your current approach. If your organization does not have such a formal structure, the section will enable you to start the process of creating one.

The structure we shall recommend is adapted from that proposed by Ansoff (1968) and can be presented diagrammatically as shown in Figure 5.

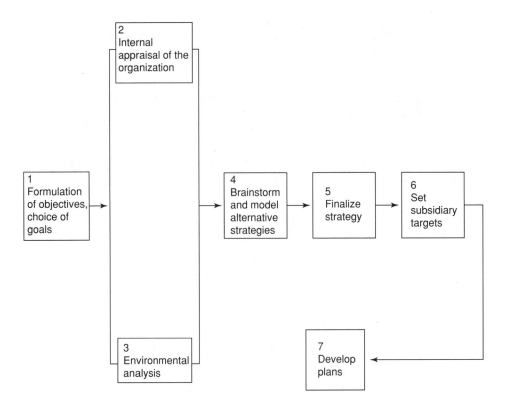

Figure 5   Strategic planning process

How does the model in Figure 5 compare with the approach to strategic
planning taken by your organization?

What are the similarities?

What are the differences?

We will now look at each stage of the model in turn.

Goals and objectives

As we have seen, there is confusion in the management literature about the use of the different terms vision (or mission), goals and objectives. Although there are no 'right' definitions of these terms, we will now propose a consistent terminology that we will follow for the remainder of this section.

- The organization's 'vision' is a statement of the broad, long-term direction in which the organization wishes to go, incorporating the values it will espouse on the way.
- 'Goals' are general statements of the tasks the organization will set itself in order to pursue its vision. Again, they relate to the long term and may be couched in language such as:
  - to maximize profit
  - to achieve growth
  - to gain or maintain brand leadership
  - to improve productivity
- 'Objectives' are finite, quantified targets that the organization sets itself to achieve within a defined time-scale.

As we will see later, the speed and discontinuity of change are such that organizations typically are reducing the time-scales applied to their strategic planning. Consequently, goals tend to be set for a three-year period, with detailed, quantified objectives set for no longer than six months or a year. Of course, these time-scales are typical, not invariable. There are still some relatively stable industries where it is both possible and necessary to plan in detail over longer periods – for the purposes of long-term investment, for example, or because, as in the case of construction, the product itself takes a long time to build. However, in rapidly changing markets, the dangers of long-term planning are obvious. Many construction companies were persuaded by the boom in housing and offices in the 1970s and early 1980s to acquire sites and build property, only to find that the crash in demand left many of them unsold and empty.

We can now look in more detail at the sort of goals which organizations set themselves. The following extract is taken from Beardshaw and Palfreman (1986):

a) *Profit maximisation. It is usually assumed that business organisations will always try to maximise their profits. This means that not only will they try to make a profit, but they will also try to make as much profit as possible. There are well-established policies to achieve and maintain profit maximisation:*

    i)   *Concentration on producing and supplying these goods and services where demand is increasing.*

    ii)   *Minimisation of the cost of production by selecting the cheapest possible combination of premises, machinery and labour to use. Thus, if substituting machines for labour is cheaper, this will be done despite the social consequences associated with the redundancies which may follow.*

    iii) *Maintaining output at the level at which profits are maximised.*

    iv) *Where a single organisation is dominant in its own area of activity, it can affect the price of the goods it produces by varying the amount it supplies to the market. It is therefore able to adjust either price or output to suit its own profit maximisation objective.*

    v)   *Research and development of new products and processes is a vital activity if a business is to survive in a changing environment ...*

b)   *Brand leadership/market domination. This may be pursued for the purposes of profit maximisation but this need not be so. Domination of a market may also give stability and security to the organisation. This might be viewed by the managers as more attractive than profit maximisation. Pursuit of this objective may lead a business to pursue a policy of sales maximisation. For example, a business might cut prices and accept losses for a time with the objective of driving its rivals out of business. Having achieved this it could then exploit the market.*

c)   *Corporate growth. Growth means increasing power and responsibility for managers, often reflected in higher salaries. Hence, this objective is obviously attractive. However, growth may be achieved at the expense of profit maximisation and therefore may not be in the interests of the owners of the organization. For example, new and less profitable goods may be produced.*

Growth can be achieved by:

    i)   *Expanding existing markets, e.g. through new products or advertising.*

    ii)   *Diversifying, i.e. extending the product range or activity of the organisation into new areas.*

    iii) *Take-over (purchasing control) of other business organisations for either of the two previous purposes.*

These goals, together with the policies or strategies to achieve them, are typical of commercial organizations. To them we can add not-for-profit goals such as 'develop self-sufficiency' (for a charity such as Oxfam), 'provide an educational and social base for success in future life' (for an educational authority) or 'provide an effective standard of secondary healthcare' (for a hospital).

ACTIVITY 42   A7

Apply the goal-setting stage of the strategic planning process to your own organization.

How would you define the goals of your organization? (This may be an opportunity to review existing goals critically, or to develop a set from scratch if they do not already exist.)

Once a set of goals is in place, they provide the basis for the development of quantified objectives within a specified time-frame. In order to be useful for performance monitoring and management control, objectives need to contain four elements.

1   an attribute, i.e. what is to be measured or achieved (e.g. return on capital, standard of service, qualifications to be gained)
2   a unit of measure, e.g. a percentage, a number
3   a quantity
4   a time limit for achievement

The application of this process will result in an objective such as:

'To achieve, by December 2000, a profit before tax on a capital employed of 15 million, through a turnover of 45 million gained in 300 retail outlets.'

'To ensure that 45% of 16-year olds gain a minimum of 5 GCSEs at grades A–C with effect from the end of the academic year 1997–98.'

ACTIVITY 43

Do your organization's objectives contain attributes, units of measure, quantities and time units?

If not, what elements are missing and what should they be?

Internal appraisal and environmental analysis

Commonly known as a SWOT analysis, standing for

Strengths
Weaknesses
Opportunities
Threats

This process sets out to identify the level of difficulty the organization will experience in achieving its objectives – in other words, the distance from where it is to where it wants to be.

At first sight, it may seem illogical to carry out the SWOT analysis after setting the organization's objectives. After all, is it not unrealistic to set the objectives without knowing first what is possible? Klinver (1978) comments as follows:

In the preceding paragraphs, the emphasis has been on the results required from the organisation in order to fulfil its basic purpose. No mention has been made of the practicability of securing these results in the short term from the organization with all its present imperfections. Indeed, this is the main reason for ensuring that the consideration of objectives comes before a close investigation of the organization's strengths and weaknesses. Too close a study of present problems before setting objectives is found to result in objectives being set too low, in a depressed acceptance that current ills are incurable.

On the other hand, it would be reckless to set objectives which have no relationship to the organisation's ability to achieve them. In practice, the stages of setting objectives and assessing capabilities go ahead at the same time, with the objectives being progressively refined as more data becomes available and more hypothesis about future operations are tested.

You may already be familiar with the process of SWOT analysis. Here, then, is a summary of the main considerations.

INTERNAL APPRAISAL – STRENGTHS AND WEAKNESSES

An internal appraisal of strengths and weaknesses should involve an objective and critical analysis of such aspects of the organization as:

- management
- labour
- products
- production methods
- distribution
- finance
- physical assets and resources
- systems
- plans
- research and development
- capital structure
- intangibles (such as goodwill or brand value)

Each of these aspects should be examined in detail. So, for example, an examination of management would include an assessment of experience, levels of skill and training, age and the effectiveness or otherwise of the organization's succession planning. An examination of physical assets and resources would include an assessment of suitability, age, cost of replacement and the level of flexibility to adapt to new products or systems. It is important to recognize that conclusions drawn from an internal appraisal should be relative, not absolute. By this we mean that all aspects of the internal operation – methods, systems and resources – should be assessed by comparison with two further factors:

1 relevance and suitability to the achievement of the organization's objectives
2 the quality and standards of other similar and competing organizations

The second factor raises the issue of inter-firm comparison or benchmarking. The virtue of establishing norms or benchmarks by surveying practice across organizations has long been recognized. In the UK, the Centre for Inter-Firm

Comparisons has been reporting regularly since the 1950s and the process of benchmarking has become a major growth industry in the USA. The Institute of Management publishes a *Management Checklist No 060* entitled 'A programme for benchmarking' to which interested readers should refer.

The benefits of making an internal appraisal relative should be obvious. While the absolute question: 'Is our workforce motivated?' may bring an answer that requires action, the further question: 'Does our workforce have the motivation to take on the challenge presented by next year's objectives?' is fundamental to the organization's likely success in achieving these objectives.

Equally, the question: 'Do our products offer good value for money?' can only be answered by reference to the value for money offered by similar products from competing organizations.

ENVIRONMENTAL ANALYSIS – OPPORTUNITIES AND THREATS

In Section 2 of this workbook, we set out the principal factors – political, economic, social, technological, legal and 'green' – and the impact they can have on organizations. In Section 3, we considered the nature of competition and the impact of changes in the marketplace.

An environmental analysis translates this awareness of what is happening in the wider world into the opportunities and threats that they present to the organization. Of course, it is somewhat artificial to try and consider each of these factors separately. A recent example is the reduction in giving to charity in the UK. This has resulted from a combination of environmental causes:

- a social phenomenon that has been called 'compassion fatigue'
- the economic considerations of job insecurity and unemployment
- competition in the shape of the National Lottery
- political inability to restore the public 'feel-good' factor

Nevertheless, despite the difficulty involved in drawing reliable conclusions from an environmental analysis, such a process remains essential for any organization that is concerned to plan for the future.

Figure 6 highlights the main elements of a SWOT analysis.

Internal appraisal (strengths and weaknesses)	Environmental analysis (opportunities and threats)
Management	Political
Labour	Economic
Products	Social
Production methods	Technological
Distribution	Legal
Finance	Environment
Physical assets	Markets
Systems	Competition
Plans	
Research and Development	
Capital structure	

Figure 6   Main elements of a SWOT analysis

ACTIVITY 44   A6.4

Now review your own organization's SWOT analysis.

Is it comprehensive?

Is it realistic?

Strategies and plans

So far, we have made no distinction between planning at a corporate level and what should be happening in individual subsidiaries, divisions or departments. In fact, a very similar process should be taking place at both a corporate and subordinate level, as Michael Armstrong (1990) exemplifies:

Managers can and should develop mission statements for their own functions, as in the following example for the personnel department of the International Stock Exchange.

The mission of the personnel department is to develop and promote the highest-quality personnel and human resource practices and initiatives in an ethical, cost-effective and timely manner to support the current and future business objectives of the International Stock Exchange, and to enable the managers to maximise the calibre, effectiveness and development of their human resources.

We shall explore the ways in which corporate and subordinate plans should be developed and integrated a little later in this section.

However, it is at this stage of the overall process that strategic planning has the greatest impact on the component parts of the business. Organizations need strategies in the following areas:

- *corporate*: long-term growth; increased profitability; product-market development; diversification; acquisition; investment and disinvestment
- *marketing*: target markets – the market segments on which the organization will concentrate and the marketing position it proposes to adopt in each segment; the marketing mix – the blend of controllable marketing variables which will produce the required response in the target markets and will include new products, prices, promotion and the placing of sales and distribution activities
- *manufacturing*: the resources required in terms of plant, equipment and any form of new technology to meet market requirements and improve quality and productivity
- *research and development*: the threat of theoretical and applied research in the light of assessed market needs; the direction in which development activities should go to support marketing and manufacturing strategies
- *personnel*: human resource management – the acquisition, motivation and development of the human resources required by the organization; organization development – the steps necessary to manage change and create a more effective organization; employee relations – creating constructive and co-operative relationships with employees
- *finance*: the acquisition and utilization of the financial resources required by the organization to its best advantage
- *data processing*: planning the information technology, hardware and software requirements of the firm to support growth and improve effectiveness

The development of strategy is self-evidently a complex process, because functional strategies are interdependent and need to be mutually consistent and supportive.

The development of individual strategies is also complicated, because it involves:

- analysing critically current strategies to assess their effectiveness and suitability to achieve the organization's objectives in the light of the internal appraisal and environmental analysis
- generating alternative strategies where necessary
- evaluating the alternatives
- selecting the best

Only when this process has been completed is it possible to set measurable targets for departments, sections and individuals so that they can formulate action plans to achieve them. For example, a marketing strategy will need advertising and promotional plans, plans for the sales force, a pricing policy and decisions on physical distribution.

ACTIVITY 45

How does your strategy development process compare with the model we have suggested?

Do any functions in your organization *not* have a formal strategy?

What structures and processes are in place for the development of strategy?

How effective are they?

Who 'does' strategy?

In a typically outspoken comment, Tom Peters (1988) says:

Sound strategic direction has never been more important – which is why the strategic planning process must be truly decentralised. Yet strategic planning, as we conventionally conceive of it, has become irrelevant or worse damaging.

What is a good strategic plan. There is none. But there is a good strategic planning process. A good strategic planning process (1) gets everyone involved, (2) is not constrained by overall corporate 'assumptions' (e.g. about the general economic picture), (3) is perpetually fresh, forcing the asking of new questions, (4) is not to be left to planners, and (5) requires lots of noodling time and vigorous debate. ...

The 'new' strategic plan, and planning process, must necessarily be 'bottom-up'. Assessing the ability (and necessary skills) to execute – to be responsive, flexible, attentive to customers – starts on the front lone. Obviously, as the process moves forward, it will involve debate among senior officers, and compromise. But it should never lose touch with or sight of the front line, where execution takes place.

Most management authors would not go that far! Nevertheless Peters' remarks are consistent with advice given extensively elsewhere. For example:

The important decisions, the decisions that really matter, are strategic... Anyone who is a manager has to make such strategic decisions. (Drucker, 1955)

I approached the matter of organization from the standpoint of a thorough belief in a decentralized organization. I still .... am just as firmly of the same belief that a decentralized organization is the only one that will develop the talent necessary to meet the Corporation's big problems. (Sloan, 1963)

In deciding where the company ideally would like to be, I believe that businesses should operate both from a bottom-up and a top-down view. Very frequently people closer to today's marketplace than to the board are more realistic about the possibilities for their business than those at the top. (Harvey-Jones, 1989)

Naturally, a consultative approach to strategic planning is considerably messier and more time-consuming than a top-down approach, where the plan is put together, either by the board or by a dedicated strategic planning team. The advantages of a top-down approach are, unfortunately, equally its shortfalls. The purpose of strategic planning is summarized in the Ansoff (1968):

Strategy is a concept of a firm's business which provides a unifying theme for all of its activities.

Consequently, a strategic plan should present an integrated, co-ordinated and consistent view of the route the organization wishes to follow. A centrally constructed plan, imposed from the top, is relatively quick and simple to make consistent, often by ignoring inconvenient data or deliberately excluding weaknesses of the business or constraints upon it. While a properly prepared plan, put together at the centre, will seek to avoid these traps, it is still incapable of leading with another, perhaps more important drawback. This is the fact that implementation of the plan will be the responsibility of line managers in operating divisions. Consequently, as *The Manager's Guidebook* points out:

No matter what the action required by the plan, there are two pre-requisites for success:

- *Responsibility for the implementation of each part must be allocated to specific members of management, who must be adequately briefed.*
- *The process of educating management and staff about all aspects of the plan, and what part they have to play, must be formally carried right down the management line. Enthusiastic commitment is the key to success.*

Such enthusiastic commitment is unlikely to result from attempts, however sophisticated, to simply 'tell or sell' the content of a centrally prepared plan. Consequently, we are left with the messy, consultative, iterative and time-consuming approach we mentioned earlier. This will involve:

- individual teams and departments reviewing their own past performance the same groups identifying their own strengths and weaknesses and forecasting the environment in which they will operate, recognizing both constraints and opportunities
- constructing individual missions, goals, strategies and plans

Of course, this is likely to result in a high degree of inconsistency. The halfway house adopted by many major organizations is for the board to publish a statement of corporate vision and strategies, and then to ask the subordinate parts of the organization to create their own strategies and plans to contribute to them. This is where a central planning team can help, by issuing guidelines for the preparation and structure of subordinate plans, co-ordinating the results and facilitating the iterative process needed to achieve ultimate consistency.

ACTIVITY 46

How much consultation and bottom-up preparation are involved in the development of your organization's strategic plan?

What concerns do you have about the degree of commitment (at all levels) to implementing the plan?

What action would be needed to make strategic planning a more widely owned process?

What structures and systems would need to be put in place to achieve this?

Strategic planning in an environment of change

There are three basic responses to change:

- ignore it
- adapt to it
- plan for it

Each of these responses has a parallel in organizational approaches to strategic planning in an environment of change and is reflected in the different cultures and structures of the organizations that adopt them.

Much of what follows is based on the chapter 'On the Cultures of Organizations' in Charles Handy's *Understanding Organisations* (Penguin, 1985).

Ignoring change totally is not a real option for any organization. There is simply too much of it about and the management literature is full of titles such as Toffler's *Future Shock*, Drucker's *Age of Discontinuity*, Peters' *Thriving on Chaos* (1988) and many others, all of which stress the speed and magnitude of change and the need for organizations to adapt effectively to it.

Nevertheless, some organizations operate in a more stable environment than others. As Handy explains:

Where the organisation can control its environment, by monopoly or oligopoly, where the market is stable or predictable or controllable, or where the product-life is a long one, then rules and procedures and programmed work will be successful. So the civil service (a monopoly in a sense), the automobile and oil industries (long product life-cycles and perhaps some oligopoly situation), life insurance companies and retail banking (long product life-cycles), are usually role cultures and successful ones.

Handy describes the structure of a role culture as being like a Greek temple as shown in Figure 7.

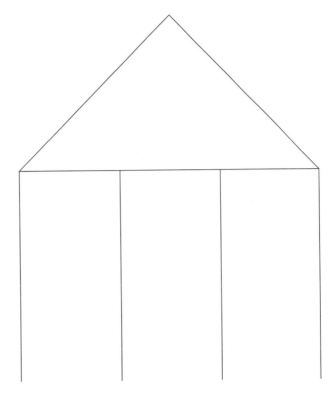

Figure 7   The Greek temple structure of a role culture

A role culture is based on logic and reason. Its strength lies in the pillars of the temple – the organization's functions, finance, purchasing, production, legal. The work of the pillars and the interaction between them, are controlled by rules and procedures – job descriptions, limits of authority, operations manuals and so on.

Role cultures offer security and predictability to the individual. They offer a predictable pattern and rate of advancement up a pillar, but they are slow to perceive the need for change and slow to change even if the need is seen. Typical responses to change in a role culture are to reorganize, redefine responsibilities and rewrite procedures. Provided that the rate of change is slow enough, such responses may work. However, rapid change means that the organization is invariably a couple of steps behind. In addition, people who joined because they were attracted by the security and predictability suddenly find that the psychological contract they thought they had no longer applies. This is a common complaint among civil servants and members of the armed forces in the UK.

In a role culture, strategic planning almost invariably follows the centrally developed, centrally imposed philosophy we have already described. Provided that year-on-year changes to the plan are minor and incremental, such an approach stands a reasonable chance of success, because it meets people's expectations of predictability and readiness to conform. Major or discontinuous change, however, brings resistance and insecurity and is inconsistent with the steady-state environment for which the role culture is designed.

Adapting to change, by contrast, involves a rapid and authoritative response. This is the prerogative of what Handy calls a 'power culture', with a structure that looks like a web as shown in Figure 8.

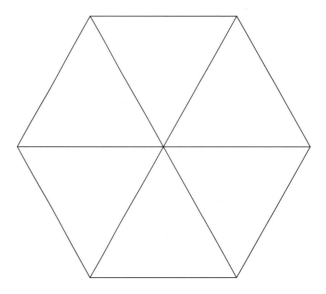

Figure 8   The web structure of a power culture

Power cultures are typical of small entrepreneurial organizations. The culture depends on a central power source, with rays of power and influence spreading out from that central figure. In a power culture, relationships are very important, communication is direct, there are few rules or procedures and the atmosphere is highly political.

They respond rapidly and positively to change because they have the ability to move quickly and can react well to threat or danger, because the person at the centre will take decisive action, give orders and make things happen.

However, the success of power cultures depends on having the right people at the centre. They are likely to fail if the quality of decision making is poor and also when the organization grows to a size where those at the centre can no longer 'keep their finger on the pulse' of everything that is happening.

Strategic planning may not happen at all in a power culture. If it does, the approach will be informal and broadbrush, allowing plenty of room to manoeuvre. The plan is unlikely to be communicated.

Planning for change is the necessary approach when organizations need the flexibility to respond effectively to major and rapid change on a large scale. As we have seen, the speed and discontinuity of change are increasing, requiring the ability to respond effectively and quickly. A role culture is not designed to do this. A power culture can only do it if it is small enough for the people at the centre to recognize the need and are good enough to make the right decisions, and if the other members of the organization are willing to jump without question when told.

In Handy's classification, the most suitable culture for this environment is the task culture, which he portrays as a net as shown in Figure 9.

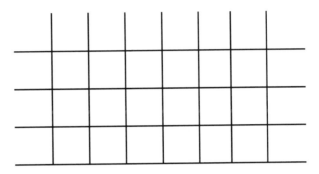

Figure 9   The net structure of a task culture

The task culture has been described variously as a 'matrix organization', a series of 'task forces' or, in US literature as 'skunk groups' or an 'adhocracy'.

A task culture succeeds by bringing together small groups of people, with the right expertise and leaving them to get on with things. It is a team culture, extremely adaptable, in which individuals have a high degree of control over their work, performance is judged by results and respect depends on ability rather than seniority or status. It is therefore appropriate where flexibility and sensitivity to the market or environment are important.

The drawbacks are an inability to exercise real control and a need for unrestricted access to resources.

ACTIVITY 47

How would you classify the culture of your organization?

Role culture

Is it suited to the size of the organization?

Yes

Is it suited to the speed of change in the environment in which you operate?

No

If the present culture is unsuitable, which would be better?

Not Power culture – we're too big
Not task – need for earlier

How might it be changed?

∴ stuck with it!

Summary

This section covered how to integrate the analysis, expanded in previous sections and developed it into coherent strategy.

Specifically, we have covered:

- the process for setting strategy
- internal environment appraisal – strengths and weaknesses
- external environment appraisal – opportunities and threats
- developing goals and objectives
- strategic planning at divisional or business unit level
- approaches in developing strategy
- culture and organization

Summary

The purpose of this workbook has been to help senior managers give a future direction to their organizations. This has involved consideration of several complementary but markedly different issues, which have fallen into two distinct categories. We can define these as 'hard' and 'soft' issues.

'Hard' issues are to do with formal analysis, the development and application of procedures and processes. The purpose of these has been to help you formulate a clear picture of where your organization is capable of going and to analyse its chances of success in taking certain directions. In order to tackle these 'hard' issues, the workbook has sought to help you develop skills and techniques necessary to:

- recognize the range of external or environmental factors likely to offer opportunities and threats to your organization
- carry out comprehensive analysis of your organization's environment
- view the products or services offered by your organization from the perspective of your actual and potential customers
- use this viewpoint to identify the nature of the competition you face
- evaluate the effectiveness of your relationships with suppliers and collaborators
- develop and apply a formal system of strategic planning
- set business objectives and targets
- develop and oversee functional plans

'Soft' issues relate primarily to people. Their inclusion is based on the recognition that, in order to operate successfully, organizations need to win the hearts as well as the minds of a wide range of communities.

In order to help you address these 'soft' issues, the workbook has sought to provide guidance on how to:

- identify all the different groups upon which your organization depends
- evaluate their current attitudes and the level of support you can expect from them
- recognize some possible causes of these attitudes
- take action to increase the level of support from your organization's stakeholders, both those with whom you have a contractual relationship and those with whom you do not
- develop a vision which will not only give strategic direction, but also gain stakeholder commitment
- identify the current culture of your organization

- recognize its suitability or otherwise to the speed and nature of the changes faced by your organization
- involve staff at all levels in taking the decisions that will affect them
- critically evaluate the relevance to your organization of some of the current thinking on staff involvement and motivation

You may have found some parts of this workbook frustrating. It has, after all, deliberately avoided presenting cut-and-dried solutions. Nevertheless, as we pointed out in our introduction, senior managers operate in an uncertain and unpredictable world. And all organizations are unique.

Consequently, we hope that the workbook has challenged you to ask some probing questions about how your organization functions. We do not claim to have given all the answers. However, we do trust that the workbook and the recommended reading that follows will enable you to find the answers for yourself.

Recommended reading

Ansoff, H.I., (1965) *Corporate Strategy*, McGraw-Hill

Ansoff, H.I., (1968) *Corporate Strategy*, Pelican

Armstrong, M., (1990) *Management Processes and Functions*, IPM

Beardshaw, J. and Palfreman, D., (1986) *The Organisation in its Environment*, Pitman

Begg, D., Fischer, S. and Dornbush, R., (1984) *Economics*, McGraw-Hill

Chismall, P.M., (1977) *European Research*, vol. 5

Coulson-Thomas, C., (1993) *Developing Directors*, McGraw-Hill

Davidson, H., (1987) *Offensive Marketing*, Penguin

Denyer, J.C., (1972) *Student's Guide to the Principles of Management*, Zeus Press

Drucker, P. (1989) *The Practice of Management*, Butterworth-Heinemann

Drucker, P., (1969) *Age of Discontinuity*, Butterworth-Heinemann

Farnham, D., (1990) *The Corporate Environment*, IPM, p.3

Friedman, M. and Friedman, R., (1979) *Free to Choose*, Avon

Galbraith, J.K., (1988) *Almost Everyone's Guide to Economics*, Penguin

Handy, C., (1984) *The Future of Work*, Blackwell

Handy, C., (1995) *The Age of Unreason*, Arrow

Handy, C., (1995) *The Empty Raincoat*, Arrow

Handy, C., (1985) *Understanding Organisations*, Penguin

Harvey-Jones, J., (1989) *Making it Happen*, Fontana

Hayek, F.A., (1969) 'The Corporation in a Democratic Society – in whose interest ought it and will it be run?' in *Business Strategy*, ed. H.I. Ansoff, Penguin

Howard, M.C., (1964) *Legal Aspects of Marketing*, McGraw-Hill

Kanter, R.M., (1989) *When Giants Learn to Dance*, Simon and Schuster

Keenan, D. and Riches, S., (1995) *Business Law*, Pitman.

Klinver, (1978) *The Manager's Guidebook*

Kurtz, D.L. and Boone, L.E., (1981) *Marketing*, The Dryden Press

Levitt, T., (1975) 'Marketing Myopia', *Harvard Business Review*, September/October

Levitt, T., (1983) 'The Globalization of Markets', *Harvard Business Review*, May/June

Lock, D. (ed) (1992) *The Gower Handbook of Management*, Gower

Martin, N., (1956) 'Differential Decisions in the Management of an Industrial Plant', *Journal of Business*, University of Chicago

Naisbitt, J., (1984) *Megatrends*, Warner Books

Naisbitt, J., (1986) *Re-inventing the Corporation*, Little Brown

Oliver, G., (1986) *Marketing Today*, Prentice-Hall

Peters, T., (1988) *Thriving on Chaos*, Macmillan

Peters, T., (1994) *Liberation Management*, Pan

Peters, T. and Waterman, R., (1982) *In Search of Excellence*, Harper and Row

Sloan, A.P., (1963) *My Years with General Motors*, Doubleday

Toffler, A., (1985) *Future Shock*, Pan

Tilles, S., (1969) 'Making Strategy Explicit' in *Business Strategy*, ed. H.I. Ansoff, Penguin

Townsend, R., (1971) *Up the Organisation*, Coronet Books

Willsmer, R.L., (1979) 'Market spectrum analysis for determining market position', *Quarterly Review of Marketing,* **5**(1), pp 1–15

About the Institute of Management

The mission of the Institute of Management (IM) is to promote the development, exercise and recognition of professional management.

The IM is the leading professional organization for managers. Its efforts and resources are devoted to ensuring the continuing development and success of its members.

At the forefront of management standards, the IM provides a range of services for its members. These include flexible training programmes and a unique range of support services such as career counselling, enquiry and research facilities and preferential prices on IM publications and other IM products.

Further details about the Institute of Management may be obtained from:

Institute of Management
Management House
Cottingham Road
Corby
Northants
NN17 1TT

Telephone 01536 204222

We need your views

We really need your views in order to make the Institue of Management Open Learning Programme an even better learning tool for you. Please take time out to complete and return this questionnaire to Tessa Gingell, Pergamon Open Learning, Linacre House, Jordan Hill, Oxford OX2 8DP.

Name:..

Address:...

....

Title of workbook:...

If applicable, please state which qualification you are studying for. If not, please describe what study you are undertaking, and with which organization or college:

....

Please grade the following out of 10 (10 being extremely good, 0 being extremely poor):

Content: .... Suitability for ability level: ....

Readability: .... Qualification coverage: ....

What did you particularly like about this workbook?

....

Are there any features you disliked about this workbook? Please identify them.

....

Are there any errors we have missed?
If so, please state page number: ....

How are you using the material? For example, as an open learning course, as a reference resource, as a training resource, etc.

....

How did you hear about the Institue of Management Open Learning Programme?:

Word of mouth: Through my tutor/trainer: Mailshot:

Other (please give details):...

Many thanks for your help in returning this form.

Institute of Management Open Learning Programme

This programme comprises seventeen workbooks, each on a core management topic with the latest management thinking, as well as a *User Guide* and a *Mentor Guide*.

Designed for self study through open learning, the workbooks cover all management experience from team building to budgeting, from the skills of self management to manage strategically for organizational success.

TITLE	ISBN	Price
The Influential Manager	0 7506 3662 9	£22.50
Managing Yourself	0 7506 3661 0	£22.50
Getting the Right People to Do the Right Job	0 7506 3660 2	£22.50
Understanding Business Process Management	0 7506 3659 9	£22.50
Customer Focus	0 7506 3663 7	£22.50
Getting TQM to Work	0 7506 3664 5	£22.50
Leading from the Front	0 7506 3665 3	£22.50
Improving Your Organization's Success	0 7506 3666 1	£22.50
Project Management	0 7506 3667 X	£22.50
Budgeting and Financial Control	0 7506 3668 8	£22.50
Effective Financial and Resource Management	0 7506 3669 6	£22.50
Developing Yourself and Your Staff	0 7506 3670 X	£22.50
Building a High Performance Team	0 7506 3671 8	£22.50
The New Model Leader	0 7506 3672 6	£22.50
Making Rational Decisions	0 7506 3673 4	£22.50
Communication	0 7506 3674 2	£22.50
Successful Information Management	0 7506 3675 0	£22.50
User Guide	0 7506 3676 9	£22.50
Mentor Guide	0 7506 3677 7	£22.50
Full set of workbooks plus *Mentor Guide* and *User Guide*	0 7506 3359 X	£370.00

To order: *(Please quote ISBNs when ordering)*

- College Orders: 01865 314333
- Account holders: 01865 314301
- Individual Purchases: 01865 314627

(Please have credit card details ready)

For further information or to request a full series brochure, please contact:
Tessa Gingell on 01865 314477